The
Therapist's
Pregnancy
Intrusion in the Analytic Space

The Therapist's Pregnancy
Intrusion in the Analytic Space

Sheri Fenster
Suzanne B. Phillips
Estelle R. G. Rapoport

THE ANALYTIC PRESS

1986   Hillsdale, NJ   London

Published by
The Analytic Press, Inc.
365 Broadway
Hillsdale, New Jersey 07642

First paperback printing 1994

Library of Congress Cataloging-in-Publication Data

Fenster, Sheri.
    The therapist's pregnancy.
    Includes bibliographies and index.
    1. Psychotherapist and patient. 2. Women psycho-
therapists. 3. Pregnancy—Psychological aspects.
I. Phillips, Suzanne B. II. Rapoport, Estelle R. G.
III. Title. [DNLM: 1. Pregnancy. 2. Professional-Patient Relations. 3. Psychotherapy. WM 420 F338t]
    RC480.8.F46   1986   616.89'14   86-17471
    ISBN 0-88163-044-6 (hc)
    ISBN 0-88163-190-6 (pbk)

Printed in the United States of America
10 9 8 7 6 5 4 3 2 1

Contents

Acknowledgments

We express gratitude to and respect for our patients, whose belief in themselves and trust in us made treatment possible. Their courage in sharing their thoughts and feelings offered us the opportunity to understand the critical significance of the analyst's pregnancy. This book represents the mutual exploration that grew out of our work together.

We thank our analysts, mentors, supervisors, professors, and colleagues who were encouraging and supportive in our endeavor. Special mention must go to Dr. George Stricker for his astute and experienced guidance from the very earliest stages and to Dr. Ruth-Jean Eisenbud for her invaluable supervision. We are indebted to Dr. Paul Stepansky, Editor-in-Chief of The Analytic Press, who believed in this book and whose enthusiastic support made it possible.

We are grateful to the psychoanalytic community (Division of Psychoanalysis, American Psychological Association) who were receptive to the presentation of our earliest ideas and observations in 1982. In addition, we are indebted to those colleagues who collaborated in the Fenster research. Their time and professional and personal involvements were invaluable in crystallizing and expanding the clinical observations and hypotheses offered here.

Last of all, we thank each other for the Friday afternoons, the bagels, the mutual respect, dedication, intellectual confrontation, joking and empathy—the unique experience of three very different people creating a book together.

Underscoring all our efforts are the sources of personal inspiration and support to which we each owe separate acknowledgment:

SF– I am grateful to my parents, who, most importantly, believed in me. I dedicate this book to my husband and partner, Jonathan Jackson, who stood by me through the long haul with tender patience, good humor, and love. Without him, and my son Daniel, this book would never have been possible.

SP– Thanks are due to my two dear little sons, my mother, sister, mother-in-law, father-in-law, and the many friends whose patience and support made the pursuit and completion of this work possible. Above all, I am grateful and inspired by my husband, Kevin J. Phillips, Ph.D. An intellectual and emotional support, he is a man who has always managed to understand my dreams and, with tireless love, has boosted me to reach for them. It is to him and our sons that I dedicate my work.

ER– I want to thank my mother for all her support. To my husband, Daniel, I give my deepest gratitude. His love, encouragement, and pride in my work are a sustaining force in my life. I dedicate this book to him and our daughters, Jessica Zoe and Leslie Zara.

Introduction

The experience of the therapist's pregnancy within the psychoanalytic situation has become a phenomenon of growing clinical concern. Before 1966, the topic had never been explicitly addressed in the literature. Prior to this time, only a single article had addressed relevant issues (Hannett, 1949), and it was restricted to consideration of the analyst's miscarriage. Beginning in 1966, with Van Leeuwen's discussion of the reactions of male patients to her pregnancy, and continuing in 1969 with Lax's treatment of issues of transference and countertransference attendant to pregnancy, new attention was focused on this phenomenon in the literature. Case consideration, clinical observations, informal research papers, and symposia are only now becoming available to those who seek help with, or are interested in, the impact of the therapist's pregnancy on the treatment and supervisory processes.

It is no wonder that the therapist's pregnancy has become an issue of clinical concern. As increasing numbers of women continue to enter the fields of psychology, psychiatry, social work, counseling and psychiatric nursing, the likelihood is great that many of these professionals will eventually become mothers. Thus, more therapists, more patients, more colleagues, more supervisors, and more training institutes will be confronted with the myriad technical, theoretical, and management issues this condition brings to the treatment situation. In addition, as more women combine professional roles with motherhood, pregnancy becomes an important social reality as well.

The issue addressed in this volume is the complex and multifaceted impact of the analyst's pregnancy on the analytic treatment process. This impact is considered in the context of the authors' clinical experiences as pregnant analysts. Our synthesis of the significance of these experiences is cast within the framework of psychoanalytic theory. Our hypotheses and observations are further illuminated by the responses and findings from a study of 22 pregnant psychotherapists (Fenster, 1983).

To gain a better understanding of the ramifications of the analyst's pregnancy on the treatment process, we must first discuss treatment as we conceptualize it. Are we referring to psychoanalysis or psychotherapy? How do we see the differences? Are these differences important to our conceptualizations about the status of pregnancy?

As the title of our volume suggests, we discuss our work as pregnant analysts within the framework of psychoanalysis. The term psychoanalysis has, of course, been open to many divergent definitions and interpretations. As early as 1941, Fenichel attempted to define and delimit psychoanalytic technique. He recognized the wide differences then existing in the field in terms of differing conceptions of what constituted proper analytic methods. He saw these differences as a function of 1) the varied personalities of analysts as expressed in their practice and 2) a lack of clarity about the principles governing all analysis, independent of differences in analysts' personality.

The traditional view of psychoanalysis begins with Freud (1914), who construed the therapeutic process as the analysis of transference and resistance in bringing unconscious material to consciousness. Change is the result of self-knowledge—making the unconscious conscious. The evolution of Freud's ideas into "classical" conceptions of psychoanalysis has come to encompass such external criteria as the use of the couch, free association, frequent sessions, the anonymity and neutrality of the analyst, and the interplay of the forces of resistance, transference, and countertransference. Within the classical setting, the analyst attempts to limit his or her personal influence in behalf of the consistently neutral formulation of interpretations.

As psychoanalytic technique has developed, there have been many expansions and redefinitions of this traditional viewpoint. Basic to these reconsiderations is the conviction that to be considered analytic a therapeutic process need not necessarily be equated with specific external criteria. As early as 1941, Fenichel wrote, "Not external measures, but the management of resistance and transference, is the criterion for estimating whether a procedure is analysis or not" (p. 23). Later, in 1945, he was more specific:

> ... whether the patient lies down or sits, whether or not certain rituals or procedures are used, does not matter. For psychotics and children as well as certain character cases, the classical method must be modified. That procedure is the best which provides the best conditions for the analytic task. A "non-classical procedure," when the classical one is not possible, remains psychoanalytic. It is meaningless to distinguish an "orthodox" psychoanalysis from an "unorthodox" one [p. 573].

In recent years, Gill (1984) has taken up this issue, distinguishing between the "intrinsic" and "extrinsic" criteria of analysis and persuasively arguing that an analytic process can be initiated and maintained if intrinsic criteria alone are met. In fact, Gill goes even further than Fenichel in proposing that analytic technique can be conceptualized—and clinically implemented—independent of extrinsic criteria altogether; technical departures, for Gill, do not achieve analytic admissibility owing strictly to circumstances in which these criteria cannot be met.

In conceptualizing the impact of pregnancy, we have adhered to this broadened vantage point in discussing issues of psychoanalytic technique. For us, psychoanalysis is in progress when there is, first and foremost, a thorough analysis of both transference and resistance, independent of such external criteria as the use of the couch, exclusive reliance on free association, frequent sessions, and a strict adherence to a neutral and anonymous stance on the part of the analyst. We conceptualize psychotherapy and psychoanalysis as a continuum. Both modalities focus on the patient's subjective inner world and personal meanings; both explore the patient's interpersonal experiences and his or her relation to the analyst. We see the essential difference between these two modalities as follows: Whereas in psychoanalysis, change is effected through a consistent and thorough analysis of transference as it gains with expression in the patient's here-and-now relationship with the analyst, in psychotherapy there is considerably less emphasis placed on the transferential aspects of the analytic relationship.

Consistent with this emphasis on the transference relationship in clinical analysis, we also hold that the analyst's influence on the patient is inevitable. Any stance, even a neutral one, is a mode of participation that tells the patient something about the analyst. Gill (1984) enlarges the traditional notion of transference to include what he calls the "inadvertent influences" of the analyst on the ongoing interactions with the patient. The analyst's personality, what the analyst attends to, the analyst's interventions and responses—both the person and behavior of the analyst—exert an undeniable but subtle influence on patterns of interpersonal interaction and, by extension, on the transference. Gill (1984) considers the notion of the "uncontaminated transference" (p. 164) to be a myth.

In contrast to the traditional view, which sees transference as a distortion determined by the patient's pathology, Gill's perspective considers transference as codetermined by the intrapsychic patterns of the patient and the influence (both intentional and unwitting) of the analyst upon the patient. Once such influence is recognized, the patient's experience of the analyst can be understood as "plausible" (Gill, 1984). In turn, the validation of the patient's perceptions of the

analyst as plausible, although not unequivocal, facilitates the patient's willingness to explore past determinants on his or her current
subjective experiences.

Maintaining the analysis of transference as the primary focus of
our work, then, we understand the value of frequent sessions, free
associations, the use of the couch, and so forth in creating an
atmosphere conducive to analytic inquiry. But, we do not believe
that modifications of these traditional criteria preclude psychoanalysis. Rather, we believe that it is the consistency with which we
attend to the patient's subjective inner world and personal meanings, in the context of an authentic and affective engagement with
the patient, that facilitates change as a function of the patient's
reconstruction of the past, self-awareness, and new affective experience.

In general, this conceptualization of psychoanalysis has heightened relevance in the current social climate, where the complexities
of life make "orthodox psychoanalysis" (Fenichel, 1945) a less
feasible therapeutic option. It addresses the conceptual quandary of
the present-day analyst who pursues the analysis of transference and
resistance, but who struggles to reconcile the inevitable life circumstances and unexpected intrusions in the analtyic space that are
anathema to traditional psychoanalytic thinking and practice. We
strongly believe that it is not unexpected events or modifications in
technique that interfere with successful analysis, but the analyst's
silence in the face of such unanticipated occurrences. External
deviations can be absorbed by the analytic process if the internal
integrity of the analysis is maintained.

There is hardly an event that so dramatically changes the analytic
space as the pregnancy of the analyst. With her pregnancy, the
analyst introduces a concrete, irreversible, and evocative impingement on the treatment setting and therapeutic dyad. The pregnancy

is an inescapable reality attesting to the analyst's real existence as a
person separate from the patient. That there are other persons in the
analyst's life—perhaps more important to her than the patient—also
becomes an unmistakable fact. The usually consistent and sheltering
quality of the analytic situation is thereby shaken at the time the
patient recognizes the analyst's pregnancy.

As the fact of pregnancy becomes ever more visible, new or
formerly buried transference—and countertransference—material
may be evoked. The "actual total personal relationship" (Stone,
1961) that subtends the transference becomes progressively accentu-
ated. New wishes, fantasies, and anxieties are engendered by the

pregnancy, for both the analyst and her patients, adding to the burden, and the promise, of analytic interaction at this time. Consciously and unconsciously, the pregnancy has an impact on analyst, patient, and technique. The inevitable interruption in the treatment process heralded by the pregnancy is one aspect of this impact; if the significance of the impending interruption is not explored and worked through, it may eventuate in premature or unresolved termination. Predictably, patients' transference feelings of loss and displacements are underscored by the reality events of the time.

Other relationships of the analyst also may change. Colleagues may feel burdened if the pregnant analyst relies on them to be available to patients or to attend to other professional responsibilities. And these colleagues too may be stirred by various feelings and reactions to the pregnancy. The collaboration between analyst and supervisor may evidence the same shifts typifying other relationships. If these shifts are articulated and explored within supervision, an understanding of their impact can provide invaluable data about intrapsychic material as well as here-and-now interactions between the pregnant analyst and her patients.

Also critical for the pregnant analyst is the need to reconcile her sense of herself as both professional woman and mother. This is especially true for first-time mothers, who must reexamine previous identifications and relationships, devaluing some, reintegrating others. Vacillation between guilt, anger, or withdrawal on one hand, and elation and a heightened sense of fulfillment on the other, may accompany this time of internal consolidation and change.

The current volume has evolved out of our personal experiences with, and concerns about, these myriad potential effects of the analyst's pregnancy. Beginning as a symposium on the pregnant analyst presented at a meeting of the Division of Psychoanalysis of the American Psychological Association, the volume brings together in one collection the points of view of clinical experience, research, and theory on the impact of the analyst's pregnancy on the psychoanalytic treatment process, on the supervisory process, and on the analyst herself.

Chapter 1 presents an overview of the existing literature on the pregnancy of the therapist. After discussing the psychological aspects of pregnancy, we review papers addressing the therapist's internal state during pregnancy, the reactions of patients, the responses of supervisors and colleagues, and research pertaining to the impact of the pregnancy on various aspects of the treatment process.

Chapter 2 provides a summary of the design and results of a study of 22 pregnant psychotherapists conducted by one of the authors (Fenster, 1983).

Chapter 3 deals directly with patients' reactions to the analyst's pregnancy, discussing transferential themes and behaviors that may be expected at this time. Patients' varying modes of recognition of the pregnancy, as well as their responses to the impending interruption of treatment, are outlined. Differences in reaction, particularly as a function of varying patient subgroups, are also discussed.

Chapter 4 concerns the analyst herself. Various countertransferential phenomena are examined across the three trimesters of pregnancy in terms of theory and clinical data.

Chapter 5 defines changes that occur in the analytic setting and the subsequent alterations in technique that are helpful in ensuring the integrity of the analytic situation and process. Issues involving the real relationship between patient and analyst, neutrality versus self-disclosure, and the increased need for interpretation—particularly of the transference—are all considered.

Chapter 6 deals with the practical and professional issues that emerge during the course of the analyst's pregnancy. We refer to such practical considerations as the disclosure of the pregnancy to patients, the issue of new referrals during pregnancy, preparing for the impending interruption in treatment, the issue of gifts, and dealing with patients' questions.

Chapter 7 discusses the treatment of the adolescent girl in light of the interacting developmental tasks of adolescence and pregnancy. Potential problem areas are outlined, such as acting out, denial, the disruption of narcissistic holding or mirroring, and the upsurge of aggressive and sexual feelings stimulated by the analyst's pregnancy. These clinical eventualities are described against the backdrop of more typical adolescent reactions that occur at this time, including the adolescent's identification with the analyst or defensively motivated attempt to "conduct business as usual." Some therapeutic directions are outlined.

Chapter 8 examines the impact of the therapist's pregnancy on the group treatment process. Drawing on the clinical material of a psychoanalytic therapy group conducted by one of the authors, the chapter considers the impact of the pregnancy on the multiple dynamics between leader, individual, and group-as-a-whole. Specific group reactions are examined with reference to of Bion's (1959) group theory and object relations theory.

Chapter 9 considers alterations in the supervisory process that may take place during the analyst's pregnancy. A unique set of relationships between analyst, supervisor, patient, and unborn baby is hypothesized. A look at how such four-way relating occurs and recommendations based on a model of parallel processes in psychotherapy and supervision are offered. The importance of supervision during the analyst's pregnancy is stressed.

Chapter 10 examines the reactions of the homosexual patient to the pregnant analyst. Considering the pregnancy to be a particularly complex and compelling event for both male and female homosexual patients, we argue for a unique interaction between the homosexual patient's intrapsychic dynamics and the event of the pregnancy drawing on both existing theories on homosexuality and extensive case material. This interaction is examined in the context of the working alliance, transference, and resistance.

Chapter 11 explores the experience of the analyst as new mother. A discussion of the intensity of the early mother-infant bond provides a backdrop for the analyst's concerns and conflicts in returning to work. A two-stage process of adjustment to work is postulated. Changes in the analyst's sensitivities, understandings, and capabilities are discussed.

It is our hope that this volume will serve as an important resource to the growing number of pregnant analysts and their supervisors. For us, the experience of becoming mothers in the context of analytic work has broadened our understanding of the human dimension of the analytic process and the analyst–patient relationship. The therapeutic situation, bearing the strain of such vicissitudes of everyday life, can offer a paradigm for what is curative: a self-integration and relatedness that allows one to meet the serendipitous with acceptance and a sense of possibility.

CHAPTER 1

Overview of
the Literature

PSYCHOLOGICAL ASPECTS OF PREGNANCY

Pregnancy is generally portrayed in the research literature as a time of emotional and psychological upheaval. Such factors as increased depression (Tobin, 1957), psychological tension (Grimm, 1961; Light and Fenster, 1974), anxiety in the first and third trimesters (Lubin, Gardener, and Roth, 1975), mood lability (Jarrahi-Zadeh, Kane, Van DeCastle, Lachenbruch, and Ewing, 1969), diminished cognitive acuity in the first trimester (Murai and Murai, 1975) and in the third trimester (Jarrahi-Zadeh et al., 1969) and altered perceptual processes (Davids, DeVault and Talmadge, 1966; Colman, 1969) have been noted.

Indeed, in much of this literature pregnancy is seen as a hurdle to be overcome, with a hoped for return to the prepregnant state of psychological equilibrium (Breen, 1975). Other studies, however, have emphasized that pregnancy is a normal developmental phase. In this view, having a child is a critical transition period for most women and couples, involving alterations in roles, values, relationships, and physiology (Benedek, 1956; Bibring, Dwyer, Huntington and Valenstein, 1961; Pines, 1972, 1982; Breen, 1975; Ballou, 1978; Entwisle and Doering, 1981). These changes are seen as ultimately calling into question old solutions and leading to new levels of intrapsychic equilibrium and organization (Breen, 1975).

For example, the research of Bibring et al. (1961) sees pregnancy as entailing a general loosening of defenses, with "the appearance of more primitive content material, and major shifts in significant relations to people and activities" (p. 26). Bibring's sample was composed solely of primiparous women (first-time mothers), and her results suggest that a first pregnancy precipitates a normal develop-

1

mental crisis during which partially resolved conflicts are revived, requiring a new intrapsychic organization of personality. The element of crisis is seen as a necessary and crucial facet of the movement from childlessness to parenthood. Crisis is seen within this framework not as pathological, but as a turning point in development. Moreover, much of the woman's psychological evolution is seen as occurring after the birth of the baby, along with the ongoing experience of motherhood.

Focusing on specific areas of flux, psychoanalytic writings on pregnancy stress the psychological pressure at this time to come to terms with one's feelings about one's mother (Deutsch, 1945; Benedek, 1956; Pines, 1972, 1982; Ballou, 1978). Benedek (1956) notes the pregnant woman's heightened dependency needs, which evoke feelings and memories of her early sense of her own mother. Pines (1982) describes a first pregnancy as an "important developmental phase in a woman's lifelong task of separation-individuation from her own mother" (p. 318). She also sees it as a "crisis point in the search for a feminine identity . . . a point of no return" (1972, p. 333). Another task involves the acceptance of the internal representation of one's sexual partner, both physically and mentally. And, finally, Pines (1972) describes the pregnancy as a "visible manifestation to the outside world that (the pregnant woman) has had a sexual relationship" (p. 334). In general, these writers stress that the turmoil of pregnancy may, indeed, facilitate the transition to motherhood, rather than merely being a peripheral symptom of the pregnant state. Ballou's research (1978) suggests a relationship between the pregnant woman's ability to reconcile her sense of her mother with her own ability to establish a sense of her child as a person. Ballou discusses changes in feminity, identity, and marital relationship. In addition, Ballou also points out that the agitation of pregnancy may facilitate the transition to parenthood.

Research regarding parity is also of interest. Many research findings indicate that although multiparous women experience a shorter and less difficult labor, first-time mothers experience most other aspects of pregnancy more positively (Winokur and Werboff, 1956; Cohen, 1966; Grimm and Venet, 1966; Doty, 1967; Westbrook, 1978). Such factors as apprehension, rejection of the child, and dissatisfaction with the wider family all increased with increasing parity. Only the fear of pregnancy and of labor was higher among primiparas. Evidence from these studies thus suggests that the adaptational tasks facing multiparas, rather than being more easily accomplished, appear to be far more psychologically profound than those of first-time mothers.

Finally, a minority of studies has found pregnancy to be a time of general emotional stability for more women when compared with matched female medical patients (Osborne, 1977), with the MMPI standardization sample (Hooke and Marks, 1962), and with a control group of nurses and student midwives (Murai and Murai, 1975). Overall, however, the majority of research confirms the presence of at least some psychological tension and depression in the pregnancies of normal women. Mood fluctuations are seen to herald adaptive developmental processes.

THE PREGNANT THERAPIST: ALTERATIONS IN SELF

It seems safe to assume that the pregnant therapist can be expected to experience many of the intrapsychic, interpersonal, emotional, and developmental changes attributed to the majority of normal pregnant women. Nevertheless, only ten articles in the literature directly address the subject of the therapist's internal state during her pregnancy (Lax, 1969; Paluszny and Poznaski, 1971; Benedek, 1973; Nadelson, Notman, Arons, and Feldman, 1974; Balsam, 1975; Baum and Herring, 1975; Schwartz, 1975; Butts and Cavenar, 1979; Barbanel, 1980; Rubin, 1980). In addition, two unpublished pieces, one by Phillips (1982) and another by Titus-Maxfield and Maxfield (1979), take an extended look at countertransference phenomena. In general, the writers cited do confirm the presence of sometimes disruptive feeling states in the therapist at this time and discuss their ramifications within the therapeutic relationship.

A process of introversion, self-absorption, and withdrawal from patients has been noted during the therapist's pregnancy (Balsam, 1975; Barbanel, 1980; Baum and Herring, 1975; Paluszny and Poznaski, 1971; Phillips, 1982; Rubin, 1980; Schwartz, 1975). A hyperawareness of physiological changes, the presence of daydreams and thoughts about the baby, and a decrease in intellectual curiosity are factors that appear to make this a more difficult time for therapists to attend fully to their patients. While most authors view this self-absorption as generally distracting from the treatment process, Nadelson et al. (1974) assert that therapists often also experience a simultaneous and paradoxical *increase* in acuity and sensitivity toward patients at this time.

Also common to therapists during pregnancy is a stance of "business as usual" (Lax, 1969; Benedek, 1973; Baum and Herring, 1975; Schwartz, 1975; Titus-Maxfield and Maxfield, 1979; Phillips, 1982). By adopting this attitude, therapists are often seen as colluding with patients and staff in denying the impact of their pregnancy on their work and professional relationships. Titus-Maxfield and Maxfield (1979) understand this mechanism of "denial" as the therapist's effort to minimize the anxiety aroused by the unknown consequences that her pregnancy brings to the therapy. For example, they would find themselves "responding to [their] own and [their] patients' anxiety by attempting to treat the baby's birth as calmly and routinely as if it had been a trip to a professional meeting or a summer vacation" (p. 5). Similarly, Lax (1969) suggests that the therapist's tendency to not "hear" patients' allusions to the pregnancy reflected a fear of the patients' hostility and—specifically with male patients—the therapist's need to maintain a "narcissistic masculine identification" as well as to avoid the "rearousal of conflicts about femininity." Lax also noted the therapist's sense of guilt because of wishes to stop work and devote her time entirely to her baby as influencing her use of "denial."

Other writers point to the therapist's heightened vulnerability, mood swings, fatigue, and emotional lability at this time (Baum & Herring, 1975; Lax, 1969; Nadelson et al., 1974; Titus-Maxfield & Maxfield, 1979). A common arena of conflict was also seen to be the therapist's feeling of inadequacy about her abilities to be a helping person because of fears regarding physical limitations (Nadelson et al., 1974; Rubin, 1980) and the difficulty of integrating the dual roles of motherhood and career (Nadelson et al., 1974; Schwartz, 1975; Butts and Cavenar, 1979).

A final area of concern noted in the literature is the clinical and personal issue of self-disclosure and exposure within the treatment setting. The therapist's pregnancy breaches the analytic custom of anonymity regarding one's personal life outside the treatment setting. Because of this breach, brought on by the therapist herself, consideration of how much the patient has a right to know, and what is best for the patient, is usual. Barbanel (1980) feels this decision depends on the patient's developmental level, and on whether the patient has siblings or children. Browning (1974) acknowledges the difficulty in knowing how much to reveal to child patients. Titus-Maxfield and Maxfield (1979) suggest that a focus on the genetic determinants of patients' reactions at this time is, in reality, the therapist's resistance to the difficult interpersonal process at hand. Changes in the therapist create tension in an otherwise reliable and consistent structure, and the therapist may react by avoiding the uncertainty of the present situation for such "knowns" as the patient's history. In addition, the therapist has heightened feelings of relatedness toward particular patients, especially mothers (Titus-Maxfield and Maxfield, 1979; Rubin, 1980).

PATIENT REACTIONS TO THE
THERAPIST'S PREGNANCY

Although the structure of the therapeutic situation emphasizes listening to the patient without necessarily requiring that the patient be concerned with the therapist, it is generally agreed that the patient can, and often will, speculate a good deal about the therapist as a person.

Stone (1961) suggests that although therapists can control the explicit and manifest communications of their feelings and opinions, it is questionable whether other gross data can be suppressed. Yet, even if her patients can discern a good deal about her under normal circumstances, the pregnant therapist *introduces* information about herself—and an alteration in the analytic frame—quite unlike the everyday "data" discussed by Stone. In this regard, then, the literature on "special events" in the life of the therapy is pertinent.

According to Weiss (1975), a special event may be "anything which alters or intrudes upon the basic analytic situation" (p. 75). Tarnower (1966), Katz (1978), and Weiss (1975) all found a strengthening of transference paradigms as a result of such special events as the chance meeting between therapist and patient, the late arrival of the therapist, the therapist's illness, and the like. Rather than distorting the analytic work, these events allow glimpses into intense feelings and fantasies about the therapist that were previously held at unconscious or preconscious levels. Especially with patients who keep the transference pale, such special events are thought to crystallize the intrapsychic clash between the therapist as a real person and as a transference figure. In addition, these authors also point out the technical errors that are potentially part of such unforeseen events and the patient's (and sometimes the therapist's) wish to return to the previous "safety and regression of the analytic situation and to the silent gratification of the transference" (Weiss, 1975, p. 75).

Given this context, then, the therapist's pregnancy may be seen as such a special event in the therapy. The writers cited below discuss some of the predominant transference paradigms attributed to this event and the resulting ramifications within the treatment and the therapeutic dyad.

Lax (1969) presents material her pregnancy elicited in six adult analytic patients. She felt that whereas her male patients used denial and isolation much of the time, the women suffered a "profound transference storm" and ultimately identified with the therapist. Positive transference reactions were not discussed. Lax also suggests that patients who are only children react quite differently from those who have siblings, although these differences were not described in detail. The most striking distinction, however, occurred between her neurotic and her borderline patients. Lax felt that her borderline patients found it much more difficult to differentiate between the transference and the reality aspects of their reactions. These patients became aware of Lax's pregnancy sooner than the neurotics and reacted "with much greater intensity," including acting-out behavior. Overall, Lax describes a process in which, with her pregnancy, the childhood situation was recreated and she was "cast in the role in which the patient originally experienced the mother" (Lax, 1969, p. 364).

In an article devoted to the patient's initial recognition of the therapist's pregnancy, Goodwin (1980) reports that women tended to "recognize" the pregnancy sooner than men, a finding that is corroborated by Bender (1975). Goodwin also found that the more intensely involved patients also "recognize" the pregnancy early. Recognition may be expressed in acting out (missed appointments, rage outbursts at siblings, pregnancy) or associative material and dreams. Questions regarding confidentiality, statements about "something queer in the room" (Benedek, 1973), and sexual concerns were also seen as signs of a patient's undisclosed recognition of the pregnancy. Also addressing the issue of recognition is Barbanel (1980), who found that in preference to accepting the possibility that she might be pregnant, patients felt more comfortable assuming the therapist was fat, was gaining weight because she was without a man, or was homosexual.

Paluszny and Poznanski (1971) described patient reactions to their pregnancies during residency training. They noted central themes of rejection, sibling rivalry, oedipal strivings, and identification with the therapist and the baby in both their adult and their child patients. While they saw temporary regressions in some patients at this time, they did not feel there were any permanent setbacks.

Nadelson et al. (1974) comment on the upsurge in patients of feelings of sexual conflict, fears of abandonment, and memories of previous loss; the revival of issues with siblings, competition; and an intensification of the ambivalent mother–child relationship in the therapeutic interaction. From their work with children, these authors cite the child's accusations that the therapist is not a good mother as putting a strain on the therapist, who is simultaneously working through her own feelings about her maternal identity. In addition, children may ask frank questions about sex or may become physically aggressive as a result of their jealousy.

The effect of the therapist's pregnancy on the treatment of children is also addressed by Browning (1974). She points to the heightened mechanisms of denial, displacement, and fears of abandonment in children. Browning advocates telling child patients as much about the baby as they want to know because, in a sense, the baby "has become part of the treatment, unlike other aspects of the therapist's personal life" (p. 481). She acknowledges, however, that it "was not always clear just where one should draw the line in terms of how much personal information to reveal" (p. 481). Certain issues, such as who will be caring for the child, seemed particularly important for her young patients to ask about and discuss in therapy and seem to reflect a displacement of personal concern. The impact of the therapist's pregnancy on a child, and especially on adolescent patients, is an area that deserves further attention.

Titus-Maxfield and Maxfield (1979) discuss patients' concerns about how the therapist's pregnancy would change their relationship with the therapist. They noted patients' wishes to be helpful and to spare the therapist further stress. Also typical was an attempt to separate the person of the therapist from the therapy, which the authors understood as patients' wishes for a return to the previous anonymity of the therapeutic situation. In addition, the authors noted that some patients wanted to leave or terminate treatment after learning of the therapist's pregnancy. This withdrawal was seen as masking powerful feelings of dependency on the therapist, which had until then gone unrecognized.

Cole (1980) discusses the reactions of three female patients to her pregnancy. In each case, the pregnancy was viewed as highlighting the patient's own dynamics and issues, as well as intensifying the experience of the transference. One patient profited from the catalytic effects of the pregnancy regarding transference material, whereas another patient terminated precipitously because of intense feelings of abandonment. A third patient used reaction formation and denial during the pregnancy but could later express feelings of loss and envy. Similarly, Bender (1975) found that patients integrate their responses according to their individual histories and conflicts.

She concluded that the pregnancy did not skew the treatment but, rather, intensified certain issues, particularly fears of abandonment. Patients commonly identified with the therapist as someone about to die or be injured.

Barbanel (1980) and Schwartz (1980) also describe the varying uses that patients make of the therapist's pregnancy, both positive and negative. Schwartz focuses her discussion particularly on the therapist who terminates with patients as a result of her pregnancy.

The differences between group and individual reactions to the therapist's pregnancy are examined by Raphael-Leff (1980) and Breen (1977), who noted family themes, sexual curiosity, and themes related to parental sexuality in their groups. In individual therapy, however, feelings of exclusion, deprivation, competition with the therapist's husband, envy of the therapist's creativity, and impingement by the outside world were expressed. Breen's sense was that the individual setting represented the early mother–baby relationship; the group setting the later child–family experiences. This does not mean that individual patients necessarily showed more primitive defenses than patients in group. Rather, the group could more easily use the defenses of denial and splitting, and the loss of the good therapist was not catastrophic. However, Breen felt that in the individual setting, the patient had to deal with ambivalent feelings toward the therapist-parent more intimately and directly.

Several authors have attempted to examine the social factors that have heretofore discouraged an examination of the therapist's pregnancy. Benedek (1973) suggests this avoidance results from pregnancy's being one aspect of a taboo subject, sexuality. Barbanel (1980) discusses the historical trend for women to hide, or not talk about, their pregnancies. She suggests that the taboo may relate to the fear that talking may result in a feared outcome (i.e., miscarriage). In addition, childbirth has, since biblical times, been associated with pain, danger, and death. Elaborate mythologies, religious rituals, and superstitions surround the event.

Clarkson (1980) also cites the many myths, and the "archaically derived and displaced elements" associated with pregnancy. In addition, she points to the "pronatalism" of our culture, which requires that a positive, approving, congratulatory attitude be maintained toward pregnancy. Negative attitudes, if they exist, may not be expressed. Clarkson feels that given such a pronatalist society, gifts from patients to the therapist are not highly inappropriate and must be seen within this context. Also regarding this issue, Benedek (1973) suggests that gifts be examined for underlying ambivalence. Clarkson concludes that "the therapist needs to be active and persistent if these underlying processes are to be reached" (p. 316).

Particularly with regard to the reactions of male patients to the therapist's pregnancy, the writings of Lax (1969), Breen (1977), Raphael-Leff (1980), van Leeuwen (1966), and Titus-Maxfield and Maxfield (1979) are pertinent. It is generally agreed that male patients react with some degree of defensive denial, isolation of affect, and suppression regarding the therapist's pregnancy, and several hypotheses have been offered in explanation. In discussing group reactions to the pregnancy, both Raphael-Leff (1980) and Breen (1977) suggest that males are precipitated by the pregnancy into a sexual identity conflict involving wishes to bear a child. They respond with a "flight into homosexual themes and interests." Blum also speculates that this may be a reaction to the "potent, sexual woman" now embodied by the pregnancy of the therapist (p. 201).

Van Leeuwen (1966) discusses the analysis of a male patient from the point of view of pregnancy envy and woman-envy. At first, regressive longings to be the analyst's baby and wishes to replace her husband were encountered. Later in the pregnancy, however, the patient began to face his more deeply repressed envy of women. The therapist was seen as the complete person "with creative strength derived from her bisexual role as a professional woman and mother" (p. 323). These feelings spurred the patient's own productivity, and his identification with the therapist enabled him to experience his own paternal feelings more acutely. Titus-Maxfield and Maxfield (1979) described men's responses that "ran the gamut from wishing to be the baby's father, to wishing to be the baby, and finally wishing to be a pregnant woman capable of becoming a mother" (p. 11).

The defensive aspect of males' behavior at this time, then, is generally seen as being precipitated by sexual conflicts regarding the therapist, sexual identity conflicts regarding male identifications, and underlying wishes to be female and pregnant. Only Phillips (1982) and Lax (1969) add that the recalcitrance seen in male patients at this time may also reflect the therapist's own discomfort in dealing with her pregnancy with these patients.

SUPERVISORS' AND COLLEAGUES' RESPONSES TO THE THERAPIST'S PREGNANCY

Butts and Cavenar (1979) suggest that the intrapsychic conflicts felt by many pregnant therapists originate in their interactions with colleagues and supervisors. Baum and Herring (1975) have suggested that the pregnant therapist may by her own feelings of guilt and anxiety provoke reactions of anxiety, jealousy, and hostility in peers and supervisors. Butts and Cavenar take the viewpoint that supervisors and peers may unwittingly create intrapsychic conflict for the pregnant therapist, and she may, in turn, react differently toward them. Butts and Cavenar suggest a more interpersonal view of the pregnant therapist's difficulties. For example, they illustrate how negative reactions from colleagues may mobilize identity conflicts, ambivalence, guilt, masochistic responses, ego-ideal conflicts, and self-defeating behavior in the therapist. In one case, the authors describe a patient who made no recognizable reference to the pregnancy. When the resident discussed bringing up her pregnancy with the patient, her supervisor felt that the patient's lack of attention was perceived by the resident as a narcissistic injury and that "the patient should pay no more attention to the pregnancy than he might new shoes or glasses that the resident might have" (Butts and Cavenar, 1979, p. 1588). Several such cases suggest the need for increased attention to peer and supervisor reactions to augment an understanding of their contributions to the therapist's difficulties.

Benedek (1973) has written about how the reactions of an inpatient staff paralleled patients' reactions to her pregnancy. In her discussion of her own plans and expectations for her patients, Benedek reports that the staff were able to recognize their own feelings about her pregnancy. This, in turn, created a freer atmosphere in which staff could help patients deal with their own feelings. Benedek sees the need for ongoing dialogues between staff and the pregnant therapist as a means of facilitating empathy with patients.

RESEARCH PERTAINING TO THE THERAPIST'S PREGNANCY

Lax (1969) and Schwartz (1975) both discuss the implications of the therapist's pregnancy by using personal and collected observations of colleagues who had been pregnant. The method of data collection, analysis of the material, and so forth was not given. The observations were presented in a narrative and descriptive format.

Spence (1973) conducted a study of one patient's train of thought (via recorded verbalizations) from her first meeting with a pregnant therapist to the meeting in which the question "Are you pregnant?" was asked. By means of a computer programmed to count words in preselected categories, Spence found that the patient used a cluster of derivatives about the pregnancy (references to bulging appearances, suspiciousness, or anger) when she was *least* likely to ask the therapist whether she was pregnant. Spence concluded that the patient's free associations were frequently in the service of resistance. They provided a linguistic disguise, which also bound the patient's associations and any emerging anxiety about the pregnancy. Moreover, because the therapist felt the patient was associating well at these points, she did not intervene to interpret.

Only two authors did systematic research about the opinions, feelings, and attitudes of pregnant therapists (Berman, 1975; Naparstek, 1976). Both studies were retrospective and placed the responses of primiparous and multiparous women together.

Naparstek (1976) mailed a questionnaire to psychotherapists who had delivered in the two years prior to the study. All had continued treatment with their patients after delivery. The respondents included psychiatric nurses, social workers, psychiatrists, and psychologists. The therapists were evenly divided among primi- and multiparas. Naparstek found that most therapists voiced surprise at the primitive, affect-laden responses of their patients, no matter what the diagnostic category. The therapists tended to feel that they overlooked or underestimated the responses of their male patients, and felt an overall decreased ability to hear anger. However, they felt generally more available and alert with their patients during the time of their pregnancies, a paradoxical finding corroborated by Barbanel (1980).

Berman (1975) retrospectively investigated "destructive" behavior and "acting out" exhibited by patients during the pregnancies of nine psychiatrists (six primiparas and three multiparas), and during a six-month control period. Each of the psychiatrists, as in Naparstek's study, had been pregnant within two years of data collection. The category of major acting out included patients' violent behavior, termination of therapy, unplanned or unexpected pregnancy, and sudden miscarriage. Less destructive forms of acting out included terminating birth control and "inappropriate" sexual behavior, such as promiscuity and homosexual contact. Berman found a general increase in the reported frequency of acting out when the therapists were pregnant, as compared with a period when they were not. She suggests that the patients most likely to present problems during the therapist's pregnancy are impulsive borderline patients. (Few schizophrenic patients were seen by these therapists because of the insight-oriented nature of their work.) Berman cautions that these results must be viewed against the backdrop of articles that have pointed to the positive or facilitating effects the therapist's pregnancy has on the treatment process.

SUMMARY

The literature on the emotional aspects of pregnancy points to a myriad of issues, feelings, and moods with which the pregnant woman must grapple to prepare for the birth of her baby. Pregnant therapists, too, may be expected to confront at least some of these emotional issues.

In addition, articles on the therapist's pregnancy suggest many common countertransference—and transference—reactions. Moreover, patients have "real" reactions to the pregnancy as well, reactions that are relatively transference free, genuine, and realistic. These also play a significant role in the total relationship between therapist and patient.

In light of these provocative articles, the next chapter outlines a research project undertaken by one of the authors (Fenster, 1983) on the subject of the therapist's first pregnancy.

The Fenster Study Longitudinal Findings on Twenty-two Pregnant Therapists

The research project described in this chapter (Fenster, 1983) was undertaken in an effort to explore systematically the impact of a first pregnancy on the therapist's sense of herself, her patients, and her supervisors. Twenty-two pregnant, psychoanalytically oriented psychotherapists were interviewed both during and after their pregnancies. The two interviews focused on the therapist's own feelings, concerns, and responses to others (patients and supervisors), as well as on her perceptions of their reaction to her. With regard to the supervisory process, each therapist's descriptions were examined for parallels to similar processes that may have occurred with patients during the pregnancy.

The study is unique; previous research either relied on informally collected observations of colleagues who had been pregnant (Lax, 1969; Schwartz, 1975) or was retrospective and combined the responses of primiparous and multiparous therapists (Berman, 1975; Naparstek, 1976). In addition, no prior research had examined either the issue of supervision in light of the therapist's pregnancy or the changing internal state of the therapist herself. The Fenster study controlled for the differences between primiparous and multiparous mothers observed in the literature (Winokur and Werboff, 1956; Cohen, 1966; Grimm and Venet, 1966; Doty, 1967; Westbrook, 1978) by limiting itself to only first-time mothers. Further, it utilized longitudinal data (current and retrospective) to provide a new slant on the information already available on the therapist's pregnancy, information that might be modified or lost when reported only in retrospect. A gap of two years postpartum (present in both Berman, 1975, and Naparstek, 1976) represents quite a significant lapse in time. The 22 therapists in this project were all interviewed during their last trimester and again within six and a half months postpartum. The data are entirely from the therapists' own points of view. Thus, to define and describe clinical phemonena, the approach used was phenomenological and exploratory rather than experimental.

METHODOLOGY

Sample

The 22 therapists were selected through a combination of formal and informal professional networks, including hospitals, postdoctoral training institutes, and referrals from colleagues. All practiced within a fifty-mile radius of a major metropolitan area. All the women who were asked to participate in the study responded affirmatively. Of the 23 who comprised the sample for the first interview, 22 completed the study. The therapists were all married and Caucasian. The average age was 34.5—the youngest woman was 29, the oldest 41. This is clearly an older group for first-time mothers. This factor may be due to the requirements for the study, which selected therapists who had already completed formal training for their respective degrees (Ph.D., M.S.W., M.D.). But the high mean maternal age may also reflect the recent trend in the general population toward later childbearing and the delay of childbearing until after training.

Another noteworthy factor about the sample was their high degree of participation in the study. All the eligible therapists who were asked to participate did so, despite the time required to be interviewed. Often the response to the fact that a study was being conducted on the subject was excitement, praise, or a request for literature or results. Many later described the interviews as stimulating, as having provided them with a focused and unusual opportunity to examine the treatment of patients in light of this important event in their own lives. A few stated that even in supervision such a concentrated overview of their pregnancies had not been realized. About a third of the therapists felt that the interviews had alerted them to some potential areas of concern with patients, areas they felt they had missed or ignored previously.

The high rate of participation may have had to do with the chance the interviews offered the therapists to air their concerns and questions in a context that promised a forum for discussion. The study thus afforded them an opportunity to focus on professional issues that interfaced sharply with quite personal ones. In addition, some women felt alone in dealing with their work with patients at this time. Participation may have been viewed as a means of overcoming their sense of isolation.

Fourteen of the therapists were licensed psychologists, five were certified social workers, and four were psychiatrists who had completed or who were completing their residency training. Fifteen of the therapists were in supervision, through psychoanalytic training institutes or privately. (Therapists in supervision at their jobs only were not counted among these 15.) All but one of the 22 therapists were in private practice; nine were also seeing patients within a hospital or clinic setting.

In summarizing their therapeutic orientation, the therapists described themselves as utilizing dynamic, insight-oriented psychotherapy. Two emphasized their reliance on family theory as well. The majority of their patients were being seen once or twice weekly. Of those patients who were expected to continue with their treatment following delivery, 14% were classified by their therapists as psychotic (including schizophrenia and major affective disorders); the remaining 86% were seen as nonpsychotics (borderlines, personality disorders, or neuroses). Seventy-five percent were female patients, 25%, male. Ninety percent were adults; 10% were adolescents or children.

Measure

Two semistructured interviews were derived from the clinical phenomena already described in previous literature on the therapist's pregnancy. A pilot study was conducted first to pretest sample questions among a group of primiparous therapists who had been pregnant within the past year. On the basis of this preliminary study, modifications of the pilot interview were made and a two-interview, longitudinal design evolved providing both current and retrospective data. The interviews tapped information in the following areas: the pregnant therapist's relations with patients and supervisor(s), her changing sense of self, and practical considerations during pregnancy. A balance between structure and freedom in the questions was sought so as to maximize the range of spontaneously reported information. Complexity of responses was welcomed.

Difficulties with this type of measure are well recognized. Respondents may wish to present themselves in a positive light and may thus unwittingly or wittingly edit the events of the present or past. Despite this drawback, it was felt that therapists would respond most favorably to a straightforward interview approach. The interviewer worked towards the evolution of a sense of rapport with the participants in the study over time, which enhanced therapist introspection and self-disclosure.

Another difficulty with this type of measure was the possibility that participation in the interviews might alter the way the therapists would normally go about handling various issues. Specifically designed to examine this potential problem, some concluding questions in the second interview provided an opportunity for each therapist to assess how her participation in the study may have affected her over time.

Finally, the longitudinal design was intended to minimize the omissions and distortions that can occur in the midst of a major life experience (first interview during pregnancy) or in remembering such an experience (second interview postpartum). An attempt was made to have each therapist return to and embellish themes discussed in the first interview.

Thus, the study attempted to define and describe the occurrence of particular clinical phenomena within the context of the therapist's pregnancy. The aim was to explore these changes as they were immersed in, rather than isolated from, the complex structure of the therapist's professional and personal world.

Procedure

It was ascertained on initial contact whether the therapist was eligible for the study; 1) this had to be the therapist's first pregnancy; 2) she had to be planning to resume work with former patients after delivery; and 3) she had to have completed her training for her degree. Condition number two was to ensure that the issues discussed by the therapists about the pregnancy were not being confounded by feelings and themes surrounding termination.

The therapists were interviewed during their last trimester and again two to seven months postpartum, after the therapist had resumed work with her patients. Interviews were approximately one to one and a half hours each.

Treatment of the Data

The interviews, which had all been tape recorded with the therapist's consent, were transcribed. Identifying data were completely removed. Ten transcripts were randomly selected and examined by the author to develop a set of categories for repetitive themes, feelings, and the like for each question asked. Using these categories and the criteria set up for placement in each category, interrater reliability was achieved for Interview 1 (.98) and for Interview 2 (.89). After acceptable reliability was achieved, the remaining transcripts were coded.

Four questions in Interview 1, which asked therapists to compare their therapeutic techniques during pregnancy with their usual techniques, were analyzed by the direct difference method for correlated samples, yielding a Student's t-ratio. All other statistics are in the form of percentages. Because each therapist gave several responses to a question, the total number of responses may far exceed the total N.

BRIEF OVERVIEW OF RESULTS

Results regarding the impact of the pregnancy on patients indicate that, overall, therapists felt there to be a distinct increase in transference feelings towards them as well as an intensification of the nontransferential, real aspects of the therapeutic relationship. Previous material and feelings reemerged and were crystallized or set in relief by the pregnancy. In addition, many therapists felt that the pregnancy brought out new or unrecognized feelings in patients (such as feelings of attachment to the treatment) as well as previously buried genetic material, memories, issues (having children, goals, etc.)

Patients who showed the earliest conscious awareness of the therapist's pregnancy were generally seen to be borderline. Both healthier and more disturbed patients tended to "notice" later or not at all. Women also tended to voice their recognition of the pregnancy before men. These patterns continued with regard to reactions to the pregnancy per se. Borderline patients were the most reactive in general, showing disruptions in many areas and often precipitating crises in or outside of the treatment. Male patients tended to utilize repressive defenses (denial, repression, avoidance, etc.) with the emergence of derivative phenomena more likely. Female patients were more reactive, particularly with regard to the issues of identifying with the therapist, envying her achievements, or wanting to compete with her. The importance of the therapist as a role model for female patients was also noteworthy in the results. Reasons for these differences between diagnostic groups and between sex of patient were hypothesized in the study.

Child and adolescent patients were generally seen as withdrawing from the therapist or, on the other hand, as increasing personal questions at this time. Acting out was also noted to intensify with adolescent patients in particular.

With regard to the impact of the pregnancy on the therapist herself, a majority turned to their peers, especially those who had already had children, for help with their patients. Over half went to the literature, finding it to be scant. Almost half the therapists admitted to being somewhat preoccupied and self-involved during the pregnancy. In turn, patients' intense resistances to exploring how the pregnancy might be affecting them—including denial, withdrawal, or acting out—were felt by the therapists to be the most difficult to handle. Alterations in the therapists' sense of themselves as professional women as a result of pregnancy and motherhood were also discussed.

Technical changes in the therapists' styles of working during the pregnancy were explored. The therapists saw themselves as (a) significantly more self-revealing with patients during the pregnancy (.01 level) and as nonsignificantly (b) more verbally active (c) more interpretive in general and (d) more interpretive of transference in particular.

A large majority of therapists felt that patients reacted quite strongly to the interruption in treatment. Reactions included minor (missed sessions, emotional withdrawal, rage) and major setbacks (hospitalizations, pregnancies, other crises). Seventy-seven percent of the therapists had at least one patient who terminated either during the pregnancy or afterwards. A majority felt that the pregnancy had played some role in these terminations. Many of those patients mentioned as most disrupted by the pregnancy were later found to have made significant therapeutic gains.

Changes in therapist's style of working after the birth of the baby were enumerated in the study. Among the changes were that the therapist adhered more closely than before to limits, such as time, fee, telephone calls, and was generally more confrontive and interpretive with patients. Other changes, including new sensitivities to developmental issues and parental concerns, were also discussed.

Of the 15 therapists in the sample who were in supervision, a large majority described changes in the supervisory relationship that occurred in tandem with the pregnancy. These changes included increased dependence on the supervisor, increased feelings of vulnerability, and feelings that the supervisor had become more disclosing, caring, or "real" as a person. Also noted were some negative changes such as therapists' feelings of withdrawal from and by their supervisors. Some parallel processes were noted.

Finally, 91% of the therapists interviewed said that their participation in the study had had an impact on them, particularly in helping them articulate and discuss intrapsychic or interpersonal issues with patients. Some stated that the interview alerted them to phenomena about which they had previously been unaware. Overall, the therapists valued the chance to talk about the issues, a factor which may account for their unusual responsiveness to the study.

A detailed elucidation of the results of the study can be found in the ensuing chapters, as well as in Fenster (1983).

CHAPTER 3

Transference Themes and Patterns of Response

For man or woman, pregnancy is a major event. It is one that developmentally, intrapsychically, interpersonally, and symbolically affects one's sense of self. It is an event bearing on issues of incorporation, differentiation, dependency, attachment, and autonomy. When the therapist becomes pregnant, the impact on the analytic process is considerable. It is an event to which a patient must respond, whether in the language of myth, fantasy, dream, defense, affect, or behavior. In a sense, the therapist's pregnancy is not only a public event, but an ever-present reality within the treatment experience. It intrudes upon the analytic barrier and remains a permanent part of the history of the analysis. Whether pregnancy is considered a special event or a distinct and separate occurrence, there is evidence that patients respond to such an alteration within the analytic frame.

This chapter focuses on the patient's response to the therapist's pregnancy. To this end, the authors consider prior literature, empirical findings obtained from a study of 22 pregnant therapists extensively interviewed before and after delivery of their first child (Fenster, 1983),[1] and case material from the authors' own experiences as pregnant therapists. Perhaps ambitious in scope, this chapter discusses affect, behavior, and themes that can be expected to emerge with patients in response to the therapist's pregnancy. It considers patients' recognition and response and the differences in these as a function of patients' sex and diagnosis. It is anticipated

---

[1]Throughout this chapter, "therapists interviewed" refers to the 22 studied in Fenster (1983).

that such a focus may further an understanding of the analytic process and, specifically, of transference issues within this process.

INITIAL REACTIONS AND RESPONSES

Fenster (1983) found that on learning or deducing the therapist's pregnancy, patients respond the most strikingly with either initial pleasure or shock. Generally, even when congratulatory feelings are the first reaction, they are quickly followed by anger and a fear of abandonment. Often, the patient's expression of pleasure and happiness for the therapist lasts for only one session; in the next session there is usually a beginning expression of both rage and fear. Patients' expressions of fear and abandonment take the form of a concern that the therapist will literally stop seeing them or a concern that she will now be emotionally unable to attend to them. Patients whose first reaction is shock also move quickly into expressed fears of abandonment. Some patients deal with those fears by an unwillingness to work in the therapy. They assume that the therapist is no longer able to provide for them. Others may wish to terminate as a way of protecting themselves from the therapist's abandonment. Or termination may be an expression of retaliation towards the therapist. The following exemplifies this type of response:

> A female patient who had been in twice weekly treatment about four months when she asked about and validated the therapist's pregnancy, responded in the next session with tears and a refusal to talk. When she finally spoke, she said that there was nothing worth saying because the treatment would now be interrupted. She felt greatly betrayed and resented trusting and sharing thoughts and feelings with someone who was planning to leave. Her panic and dependence, she claimed, would force her to stay but she could not work.

Concurrent with the fear of abandonment is anger, hostility, even outrage that the therapist did not tell the patients she was planning to become pregnant. There is anger that the therapist is not going to be there for them, and anger at their own dependence on her. This is counterbalanced by the patient's discomfort with aggression towards the therapist and her baby. There is a feeling that it is not acceptable to be angry with someone who is pregnant. Patients often fear that any display of negative feelings may hurt the therapist and, in some magical way, her baby. Underlying this fear may be the unconscious wish to harm the baby and spoil the experience for the therapist. Reflecting such unconscious hostility is one patient's response to her therapist's pregnancy which included descriptions of the nightmar-ish deliveries of her own three children, leading to brain damage in one and near death for another. Often related to negative feelings is some degree of envy and jealousy—envy at the therapist for "having it all," career, marriage, and now baby; and jealousy of the relation-ship the therapist has with her husband and unborn baby.

Some patients react differently with solicitousness, tenderness, and helpfulness. These positive reactions may be seen as genuine caring responses, which bring patient and therapist closer together, or in some cases as defensive responses to the negative feelings described above.

Other initial reactions to the therapist's pregnancy include flight into health, idealization or devaluation of the therapist, intense feelings of humiliation or betrayal, and acting out in the form of missed sessions, cancellations, terminations, pregnancies, and abor-tions.

THEMES AND ISSUES

There is a degree of consistency in the themes and issues that emerge in treatment when the therapist is pregnant. These themes emerge in response to the here-and-now, real situation of the therapist, yet they are inevitably colored by the more unconscious, dynamically deter-mined aspects of the transference. Underscored by the patient's own dynamics and history is an increased focus on sexual themes, identity themes, themes regarding siblings, and issues of trust, of abandonment, of secrets being withheld. There is often some reflec-tion on the movement from a dyadic relationship with the therapist to a triadic one with therapist, the patient, and the baby. This brings to consciousness issues regarding the triangle of mother, father, and baby.

The authors' findings regarding the emergence of some such themes are corroborated by earlier literature. Paluszny and Poznanski (1971) noted themes of rejection, sibling rivalry, oedipal strivings, and identification with the therapist and baby in both adult and child patients. Nadelson et. al (1974) reported similar issues of sexual conflict, fears of abandonment, memories of pre-vious loss, as well as a revival of issues related to siblings, competi-tion, and mother–child relationships. Breen (1977) reported feelings and themes of exclusion, deprivation, competition, envy, and im-pingement by the outside world upon the analytic situation.

The authors have found that, in many cases, the pregnancy both elicits new material and themes and at the same focuses and crystallizes old ones. This is corroborated by Bender (1975), who found that patients integrate their response to the pregnancy according to their individual histories and conflicts. Similarly, Cole (1980) views the pregnancy as heightening each patient's own dynamics and issues as well as intensifying the experience of transference.

There is evidence, as reported by 95% of the pregnant therapists interviewed, that the pregnancy enhances the progress of treatment. Its impact is reflected in the intensification and elaboration of positive transference themes, the evocation of repressed material, and the stimulation of formerly suppressed material regarding pregnancies, abortions, and adoptions. The positive effects noted are a function of the in vivo experience, which demands an emotional response in the examination, symbolization and, in some cases, recapitulation of an intense situation.

RECOGNITION RESPONSE

The point in therapy at which the pregnancy first emerges as an issue for patients comes with their awareness that there is a pregnancy. Essential to a consideration of this is the patient's recognition response.

Patients use their own styles and reflect their own dynamics in recognizing and acknowledging a pregnancy. Some directly ask the therapist about the pregnancy; some allude to it through dream material or other derivatives like content themes of abandonment, children, weight gain, secrets in the room, something being unusual or queer. Others respond to the pregnancy by acting out with missed appointments, rage outbursts, sexual promiscuity, telephone calls to the therapist, silent sessions, or premature termination.

Eighty-seven percent of the pregnant therapists interviewed made a prior decision to wait for patients to recognize the pregnancy rather than inform them about it. This position involved waiting for the patients to ask directly about the pregnancy or to show derivatives of some unconscious recognition of the pregnancy through dream material or a focus on specific themes. The rationale for this position was the desire not to impose the therapist's personal event prematurely on the treatment situation. There is the assumption that when patients come to the realization by themselves, they may be more ready to deal with the pregnancy and its ramifications.

Recognition or denial of the pregnancy, then, allows for exploration of transferential or historical material. Supporting this idea, Goodwin (1980) notes that the advantage of allowing patients to use their own personal styles in recognizing the pregnancy is the wealth of information it makes available. She maintains that the recognition session is comparable to dream material in enabling an understanding of the patient's transference position and central conflicts. This is exemplified in the following case:

> A female patient who had been in twice weekly treatment a year and a half at the time of the pregnancy did not ask the therapist about the pregnancy or allude to it until the end of the fifth month. A month earlier, she had reported a dream, the sense of which was that there was something being held secret within the analysis: "In this dream I have the feeling of losing something, something I was never going to get again and I don't know what it is. In the dream I am after a man, then I am mad at L. [husband]. I am tired of being married. In the dream I am fighting with him, and he is very unresponsive to me. We fight and talk about getting a divorce. Then I am in Florida. It seems I have moved there, gone off to live with some woman." The patient's association to the dream was, "I feel that I am around someone who isn't really around me."

At this time it seems that the patient is unconsciously responding to the therapist's secret (the pregnancy). The patient has resisted conscious awareness of the therapist's pregnancy up to this point. However, her anger, fear of loss, and awareness that there is an unexplained agenda between her and the therapist are underlying themes of the dream. The sense of loss, the sense of an important person being "unresponsive," not "really around," is both historical and transferential. The patient's associations to the dream reveal the sense of being around a mother who was not there for her through most of her childhood. Being the youngest child and reportedly unwanted by her parents, she remained aloof and uninvolved as a way of protecting herself from mother's rejection and distance. Accordingly, the patient's reticence about observing or responding to the pregnancy is a function of her transference to the therapist, her assumption of not being worthy of notice and therefore of not being entitled to know. When the therapist considered the dream in terms of the transference, questioning the patient about the "secret" within the analysis, the patient responded by asking about the possibility of the therapist's pregnancy.

RECOGNITION AND RESPONSE AS A FUNCTION OF PATIENT'S SEX

A significant factor in the consideration of both a patient's recognition and response to the pregnancy of the therapist is the patient's sex. The authors found that female patients, especially those who were mothers or wanted children, were more likely than male patients to respond earlier and more directly to the therapist's pregnancy (Fenster, 1983). Male patients tended to wait and, rather than inquiring directly, responded in the form of dreams or derivative themes related to the pregnancy. There is some evidence (Spence, 1973) that the production of such derivatives actually makes it less likely that the patient will ask whether or not the therapist is pregnant.

Whether female patients actually "notice" the pregnancy before male patients is unclear. The therapist may seem different to *both* male and female patients, but in some intangible way. However, female patients, particularly those who are already mothers or are trying to become pregnant, have a frame of reference for identifying this intangible difference in the therapist. Male patients may be unaware that the changes they consciously and preconsciously note are actually manifestations of the state of pregnancy. The bond of femaleness between the female patient and her therapist may, in fact, evoke recognition.

From a psychoanalytic perspective, the male patient's failure to recognize or directly confront the pregnancy of the therapist may be a function of his early developmental movement away from a maternal female identification. It has been postulated (Greenson, 1968; Stoller, 1974) that the male infant must break from the primal symbiosis with mother in order to achieve a sense of himself as male. Unlike the female, whose identification with mother augments her sense of self as a female later on, the male must disidentify from mother and identify instead with father.

The male patient, then, may need to remain unaware or actively suppress recognition of the therapist's pregnancy in order to provide distance from the therapist's emerging femaleness. "Not noticing" may actually protect against the eruption of early wishes and experiences of being one with mother and mother's femaleness. Whereas this dynamic probably operates within any treatment situation between a male patient and a female therapist, it must reach heightened proportions when the therapist becomes pregnant.

Another facet in the male patient's nonrecognition of the therapist's pregnancy is the issue of the therapist's now evident sexuality. Awareness of the pregnancy establishes the unmistakable fact that the therapist is an actively sexual person with a male in her life.

The following example points to the possible underlying sexual issues in the male patient's reaction to the therapist's pregnancy. It demonstrates how eventual recognition of the therapist's sexuality is progressive and may be therapeutic to the male patient.

R, a 33-year-old male, had been in twice weekly treatment about two and a half years at the time of the pregnancy. He had come into treament with a complaint of colitis, a symptom of his inability to show rage and of his frustration in a marital situation. When he began treatment, his then-wife was having an affair and being very obvious about it, not returning home at night, and always being away from the house. This patient, for at least the first year of the treatment, persisted in denying his wife's sexual involvement with other men. Over the course of the treatment he was divorced, became depressed for a time, and then resumed more productive relationships with other women.

In the same session in which he asked about the therapist's pregnancy with the question "Those aren't maternity clothes, are they?" he brought in the information that his ex-wife had been having an affair during their marriage. The pregnancy seemed to have jolted the patient into facing the sexuality of the women in his life. More specifically, within that session during which the therapist confirmed her pregnancy, R responded by saying, "You're kidding. I can't believe you're pregnant. You can't be pregnant. You don't have sex. Was this an immaculate conception? No okay, I know it happened once."

In the next session, R reported being very "shook up" by the therapist's pregnancy and, in the same way, "shook up" by the information about his ex-wife. This puzzled him, since it had been at least a year and a half since his divorce. The therapist was able to make use of the connection between herself and the ex-wife to explore R's desire to deny the sexuality of the women in his life as a way of defending against oedipal fears and conflicts.

Male Patients' Responses

Even beyond recognition, male and female patients tend to respond differently over the course of the therapist's pregnancy. It has been reported (Van Leewen, 1966; Lax, 1969; Breen, 1977), and corroborated by the authors' experiences and findings (Fenster, 1983), that male patients react to the therapist's pregnancy with some degree of denial, isolation of affect, and suppression of thoughts and feelings. Male patients seem generally less willing than female patients to entertain transference issues related to the pregnancy. Men often insist that the pregnancy does not effect them; they avoid the topic and focus instead on the concrete details of the event, such as upcoming schedule changes or termination.

Evidence of their unexpressed and unanalyzed feelings is found in increased acting out by male patients in the form of missed sessions, forgetting things in the office, and even termination. One of the authors reports that all three patients who terminated upon her return from delivering the baby were male. The dreams and theme derivatives in conjunction with this acting out suggest feelings of rage, envy, deprivation, and exclusion. There are feelings of exclusion not only in the presence of the baby, but in the implied presence of another male. The authors found that issues of sexuality appear only infrequently with male patients. When reported, however, they generally involve the male patient's disgust that the therapist is no longer an acceptable sexual object or disbelief and disappointment that she is sexually involved with another man. One male patient, a few sessions after the one in which he asked about the therapist's pregnancy, commented: "You really look pregnant. You are no longer a lot of what I thought you were. I see nothing sexual in pregnant women." When the comment was explored, the patient responded with anger and a feeling of betrayal that the therapist could no longer be a sexual object because she was pregnant.

It is particularly important to consider the therapist's role in the underlying dynamics of the patient's response. From a countertransference perspective, the pregnant therapist's feelings of self-consciousness, anxiety, and guilt may interfere with a more direct examination and confrontation of male patients' feelings and thoughts. The therapist's reluctance to confront may actually complement the patient's hesitancy. As a result, the male patient may have to distance with contempt, avoidance, acting out, or even termination. From a cognitive perspective, the cultural and intellectual oversight given male envy, particularly envy of woman's procreative function, contributes to the therapist's ineffective handling of male responses. This oversight, in effect, leaves the therapist without a theoretical frame for understanding many male reactions or nonreactions.

Female Patients' Responses

The authors found that female patients most often react to the therapist's pregnancy with identification, competition, and envy (Fenster, 1983). The wish to identify with the therapist reflects different dynamics for different patients. For some, there is the need to view the therapist as a role model whose behavior implies that marriage is acceptable, that child-bearing is safe, and that the combination of career, marriage, and children is possible. In such cases, positive reassuring aspects often run parallel with the tendency to idealize the therapist.

For other patients, notably mothers, the therapist's pregnancy provides them with a ground of commonality. As such, it increases intimacy and reduces fears and inhibitions in responding to the therapist. Some patients act on the wish to proffer advice and mother the therapist, often a significant alteration in the transference. For other women, although identification is a readily available, almost automatic response, it may actually be an avoidance of the expression and experience of negative feelings toward the pregnant therapist.

The negative effect of this identification is recognized in findings of an increased incidence of unrealistic pregnancy wishes and some actual pregnancies (Fenster, 1983). Such acting out through identification may involve a wish to compete with the therapist; a counter-dependent message of "I don't need you anyway, I can do it too"; or an attempt to ward off loss of the therapist by becoming like her.

Other reactions of female patients to the pregnant therapist include envy and jealousy. Theoretically, (Riviere, 1932; Klein, 1957; Segal, 1964), envy and jealousy are considered to have different meanings. Envy is seen as a two-person situation that involves the desire for some possession or quality of the object. Often, the aim is to spoil or destroy. Envy is therefore considered a more primitive and more malevolent emotion than jealousy, which is generally related to love and involves a "triangle" in which the aim is to possess the love object and remove the rival (Segal, 1964).

Envy is generally expressed in the feeling that the therapist has "everything"—a profession, a man, and now a baby—while the patient has nothing. Patients report feelings of resentment, emptiness, and despair that they will never have it all. Jealousy expressed to the pregnant therapist is often directed at the relationship the therapist has with her husband and baby. Patients describe a sense of being replaced in importance by the real baby and having to grow up. There is jealousy that this baby will have the good mother they want. A few female patients, when exploring their wish for the therapist to have a male child, recognize their need to maintain their place as the "baby girl." Such feelings are reflected in the following example:

> P, a 50-year-old married woman, was in analysis (three times weekly) for four years at the time of the therapist's pregnancy. This patient recognized the pregnancy in the first trimester. In the second trimester, after the therapist had been away on vacation for a week, the patient left a message with the therapist's service that she was going to fall apart and that she needed to be admitted to a hospital. When the therapist called, the patient reported that with both her husband and her therapist away she had found she could not tolerate the "lack of connection." When asked about the connection with her own chil-

dren, P insisted they did not count. She wanted a connection where she was the infant and someone else was the parent. Expressing her anger, P insisted that since the pregnancy, the connection with the therapist was no longer the same. During the last session before the therapist's vacation, the patient gave the therapist a note in which she described herself as a flower, "wilted and falling" from the vine, as compared with the baby, who was the "new pink bud" that was growing. The note reflected the patient's rage at being replaced by the baby and her desire to regress to the place she had been in when she began treatment, so that she could once again be the new baby to the therapist. In the week that followed the therapist's return from vacation, there were continual phone calls by P, a return of her phobias, a refusal to use her husband as a resource, an increase in panic attacks, and generally a regression to an earlier time in treatment.

With regard to the issue of envy, the authors found that the wish to destroy or spoil the envied object, the baby, was seldom directly verbalized. There was, however, considerable evidence of defenses *against* such wishes—idealization of therapist and baby, flight to other relationships, devaluation of self or therapist, solicitousness, and the need to make reparation (Klein, 1957). Resorting to such defenses occurs because the patient fears that the expression of these wishes will lead to the therapist's retaliation in the form of abandonment, counterattack, or both. The therapist's own defense against being the object of the patient's poisonous wishes may also contribute to the lack of direct expression by patients.

RECOGNITION AND RESPONSE AS A FUNCTION OF PATIENT'S DIAGNOSIS

The literature, clinical observations, and research findings (Lax, 1969; Fenster, 1983) suggest with a fair amount of consistency that how patients deal with the pregnancy is greatly affected by their diagnosis or level of ego strength. Sixty-one percent of the pregnant therapists interviewed maintained that diagnosis was the single most important factor in determining a patient's response to the pregnancy.

These findings shed particular light on borderline patients, who as a group are strikingly similar and visible in their reactions to the pregnant therapist. Borderline patients are defined here as those patients who have in common certain symptom constellations: diffuse anxiety; ego weakness manifested by multiple phobias and a tendency to impulsive behaviors; primitive defensive operations as projection, denial, splitting; a pathology of object relations resulting from only partially differentiated self and object images and the lack of integration of libidinal and aggressive self and object images; and a condensation of pregenital and genital aims under the overriding influence of pregenital aggressive needs (Kernberg, 1975).

Lax (1969) felt that her borderline patients became aware of the pregnancy sooner than other patients, reacted with greater intensity (including acting-out behavior), and found it much more difficult to differentiate between the transference and the reality aspects of their reactions. Similarly, the authors found that patients falling within the borderline range of pathology were earlier than others to voice their conviction that the therapist must be pregnant. Often these patients had intense reactions by the second or third month of the pregnancy, long before any obvious physical changes offer clues. Notably less disturbed patients (i.e. neurotic range) and very disturbed patients (i.e. psychotic range) generally did not recognize the pregnancy as readily, if at all (Fenster, 1983).

We suggest that perhaps the borderlines' early recognition is a function of their sensitivity to the therapist's emotional stance in the first trimester. "The withdrawing from the object world and libidinal investment in self," which is said to characterize a woman in the first trimester (Pines, 1972, p. 334), may affect the pregnant therapist's usual analytic position. Noticeable changes occur daily within the treatment setting. The therapist may sit differently, become more passive or active, more verbal, and so forth. For the borderline patient, who is often described as having only partial ability to differentiate between self and object, such changes may be immediately felt and registered within the self system. Moreover, conflicts surrounding separation-individuation often lead borderline patients to be exquisitely attuned to situations that may precipitate feelings of abandonment and aloneness. The pregnancy of the therapist certainly poses such a threat. When one of the authors was about two weeks pregnant, a female patient reported this dream: "T bought a houseboat without telling me. He took a loan. He didn't even consult me. I threw him on the floor and his head became wire." Shortly after this, the patient, a borderline woman who was extremely symbiotic in her demands, had an exacerbation of phobic symptoms. The dream reflects not only her anger with the therapist but her awareness of the therapist's absorption and involvement in an issue that excluded her.

Related to this hypersensitivity, Krohn (1974) noted that the borderline's lack of cohesive object images—a characteristic that virtually defines the term borderline—enhances the borderline's sensitivity to affective states and unconscious content of others. In fact, the borderline is hypersensitive to the momentary feeling states of other people. These perceptions of others remain unmodified owing to the absence of those integrated and constant object representations that buffer such momentary shifts. Neurotics, on the other hand, register the underlying feeling states of others preconsciously, employing repression and secondary defenses to bar certain trends from consciousness. They thereby preserve the more stable representation of the object and remain relatively unthreatened by slight changes in the mood or appearance of others.

In reaction to the therapist's pregnancy, borderline patients evidence more acting out, crises, clinging, rage, emotional withdrawal, and abandonment fears than other patients. Needing an idealized object with which to merge, they seem to respond to any alteration in the treatment setting with feelings of deprivation, betrayal and rage. The following exemplifes this:

> One patient prefaced her question about the therapist's pregnancy with the comment, "I can't tell you what an upsetting thought it would be if you really were pregnant." When the therapist confirmed that she was indeed pregnant, the patient responded to the news by insisting that the therapist could no longer care for her. In the next session the patient reported the following dream: "I'm speaking with you [therapist]. I was in crisis, and you couldn't be there. I had a staff member there, a hippy guy. He hugged me and I felt better and better." Such a reaction, even in the form of a dream, reflects the immediate assumption that the pregnant therapist, no longer the idealized mother, will be unable to care for her. There is an experience of crisis and a need to replace the now ungiving mother with another, more nurturing love object.

Of those patients who terminated treatment abruptly during the therapist's pregnancy, most were considered by their therapists to be within the borderline category (Fenster, 1983). Although these patients voiced anger at issues other than the pregnancy as reasons for their termination, it is possible that the patients terminated because they could no longer use the therapist as a container for their ventilated rage. Under the circumstances of the pregnancy, the therapist had changed, and their rage had become emotionally intolerable.

OTHER REACTIONS

A patient response that is difficult to deal with is the patient's failure or refusal to react overtly to the therapist's pregnancy. This creates considerable anxiety for the therapist, who is caught between taking a nonanalytic position (and imposing her own agenda by asking questions or even confronting the patient about the pregnancy)—or remaining silent and thus in a sense colluding in the denial of a shared reality. The authors and the majority of therapists interviewed (Fenster, 1983) dealt with this by eventually explicitly bringing the pregnancy to light, especially if the patient had not recognized or responded to the pregnancy by the sixth month.

Some patients, particularly males, respond to the therapist's final disclosure with a terrible sense of humiliation at not having "seen" the pregnancy earlier. Their humiliation may be complicated by their transferential wish to be the only man in the therapist's life. The reality of the pregnancy is experienced as a narcissistic wound, and they are left with rage and despair. Narcissistic patients experience their failure to notice as "How could you do this to me?", "How could I let you do this?", or "How could I not know?"

Many overtly nonresponsive patients "know" but feel it too intrusive to ask the therapist about the pregnancy (Fenster, 1983). It may be that their reluctance to intrude is an attempt to maintain the analytic frame, which has already been intruded upon by the therapist. Patients are no longer in a dyadic situation with the analyst, but rather must deal with a third person within the analytic frame. They must deal with the reality of the therapist as a person, with an outside separate life and a sexual relationship, and may need to avoid the resentment, hostility and fear that they may actually feel. Patients must come to terms with the disclosure embodied in the therapist's pregnancy and with having been catapulted into the therapist's private world.

Related to this is a phenomenon described by Gillman (1980) as "undisguised transference dreams." In his consideration of dreams in which the analyst appears as himself or herself, Gillman notes that patients often have undisguised transference dreams related to a break in the analytic barrier, as a defense against the emerging transference neurosis, or as a specific character defense. The therapist's pregnancy certainly constitutes a break in the analytic barrier. The growing presence of the therapist in patients' dreams may reflect an attempt to ward off the trauma of the therapist's disclosure, to reconcile with the impact of her presence as a real person, and possibly as a defense against the intimacy associated with disclosure. In relation to this, the authors found that there is also an increased presence of the therapist's husband in dreams, which may further reflect the patient's attempt to reconcile with the real world relationship of the pregnant therapist. Also reflective of this are patients' dreams of being in the home, or somehow stepping into the world, of the therapist. Within the following case is an example of an undisguised transference dream:

T, a male patient of 42, was in twice weekly analysis for two and a half years at the time of pregnancy. He recognized the pregnancy in the fifth month. Two months later, the patient reported this dream: "I was knocking on the door of a brick ranch house, and every time I touched the mailbox, a little girl would say, 'Who is it?' and I would run away. It was very frightening. I heard the door open, but I never saw the little girl. I was very scared. Then you came out. I didn't say anything. There was no intended harrassment on my part—in the dream I had to do this."

In exploring the associations to this dream, the patient resisted the transferential connection, that is, the brick home of the therapist and the pregnancy of the therapist reflected in the presence of the little girl. He reported that he could not understand what the therapist "was doing there!" The dream reflects his wish to make a closer connection with the therapist by seeking entrance to her private life, the frightened position this places him in, and his anger about it. The denial of any responsibility, the insistence of "having to do this," of "having no choice," defends against the wish to enter the therapist's life and the guilt this generates. The pregnancy creates an emotional dilemma for the patient because it intrudes upon the treatment with the fulfillment of this hidden wish.

THE IMPACT OF THE PREGNANCY—POSITIVE AND NEGATIVE

For some patients their therapist's pregnancy makes treatment impossible, and they terminate. The authors, as well as 77% of the therapists interviewed, had patients who terminated unexpectedly during the pregnancy or afterwards. For some, the pregnancy was used as a resistance to treatment, which would have ended for other reasons had the pregnancy not emerged. For others, there was an understanding of the dynamics involved in the wish to terminate but an inability to get past them; and in some cases, neither patient nor therapist parted with a clear understanding of why the treatment had ended.

Such terminations notwithstanding, the authors, and 95% of the therapists interviewed, felt that overall the issues that emerged as the result of the therapist's pregnancy enhanced the progress of the treatment. On the most overt level, the pregnancy prompted discussion of important material such as secrets, childhood, parents, siblings, mother's pregnancy, prior personal pregnancies, abortions, and the like. For some patients, this meant tapping formerly repressed or suppressed memories and material. For others, as reported by 74% of the therapists interviewed, the pregnancy focused, enlivened or crystallized already existing material and themes.

Like the authors, 88% of the therapists interviewed found that the pregnancy underlined and advanced transference issues. The reality of the therapist's pregnancy places her—and the patient in response to her—at center stage. This intensifies the treatment, because it heightens an awareness and expression of conflicts and such feelings as dependency, competition, envy, devaluation, idealization, and rage for the therapist. The pregnancy makes resistance to dealing with the therapist more difficult. When considering transference issues, it is almost impossible to separate out the response to the "real" person of the therapist and the "projected nonobjective image" of therapist as transference object. The therapist's pregnancy thus seems to extend *both* the real and the transferential aspects of the treatment.

An example of this extension is the intensification of transference material relating to the therapist as a maternal object. The therapist may become the idealized mother, the sexual mother, the abandoning mother, depending on what she sets in motion within the patient's own context.

> In the case of one 36-year-old female patient, for example, the therapist's pregnancy was experienced within the historical context of a mother who had died of cancer less than a year after the birth of the patient's younger brother. The patient accordingly reacted to the pregnancy with expressed fear of being abandoned and concern for the therapist. Two weeks after she had validated her assumption that the therapist was pregnant, she began feeling physically depressed, crying within and outside the sessions, feeling a need to maintain distance from the therapist while at the same time experiencing panic that the therapist would not return. In response to her feelings, the patient insisted that she should reduce her sessions from twice to once a week—a decision reflecting her need to close the door and leave the therapist before the therapist left her. The patient stressed that the situation would be resolved for her only when the therapist had the baby and returned. The strong transference response of this patient exposed hidden fears and conflicts that intensified the analysis and enabled considerable growth.

Part of the enhancement of the transference is the intensification of feelings expressed by patients. Easily noted were genuinely caring responses toward the therapist (Fenster, 1983). One therapist, describing a patient who had been extremely nurturing to her, saw these feelings as moving both along in a positive direction: "She had idealized me to such an extent that it was somewhat of a problem at times, and I think that her being able to share an experience with me that's so blatant and concrete was particularly helpful to her" (p. 84).

The positive aspects of a maternal attitude toward the therapist
seemed to be particularly prominent with older female patients who
were mothers. Having difficulty with their position of dependency
vis-à-vis the therapist, they welcomed the opportunity to turn the
tables, as it were, and feel able to give to the therapist. Therapists
remarked on these reparative moments of concern as deeply recognized and felt by themselves, moments that very often sustained the
relationship while allowing for less defensiveness and mutual exploration of formerly hidden intimidation, envy, or angry feelings
(Fenster, 1983).

Although more anxiety producing, the intensification of turbu-
lent, angry, or negative feelings in patients did not seem to preclude
treatment gains. This was particularly true when the pregnant therapist was able to view the patient's response, although difficult and
frightening, as intrinsic to the transference, requiring confrontation,
interpretation, and firm management. In this light, many patients
who were at first perceived as most disrupted by the pregnancy were
later cited as having progressed most significantly as a result of the
pregnancy (Fenster, 1983).

Exemplifying the positive impact of a pregnancy on a patient's
reaction to treatment is the case of V:

> V was 21 years old and had been in twice weekly treatment for three
> years. She was a constricted, depressed, obsessive woman who
> seemed to live in a state of unrelieved mourning. Orphaned at 13, she
> had lived with a married brother during her adolescence. She eventu-
> ally fought with him and moved out. V did not spontaneously reveal
> any awareness of the therapist's pregnancy and seemed surprised
> when told of it at the end of the fifth month. Her initial reaction was a
> socially appropriate congratulation and generally positive statements.
> Because V did not easily share feelings, the therapist frequently had to
> wonder aloud about V's reaction to the pregnancy and the fact that the
> therapist would be away temporarily. The therapist felt the issue of
> loss was so central here that she actively pursued V's reactions. Two
> weeks after the patient became aware of the pregnancy she reported
> the following dream:
>
> "My boyfriend went to the real estate board. He spoke to the
> landlord and said, 'You better give her that apartment.' The landlord
> brought the rent down and made someone else move out to give me
> the apartment." V's association led to her concern about being pushed
> out of the therapy and brought back a series of memories from the year
> after her mother's death. Prior to this time, V had had almost total
> amnesia for that year. Her first memory of it was of her sister's giving
> birth to V's new nephew and how withdrawn, left out, and unwanted
> V felt.

She also remembered that, almost anorexic, she had stopped menstruating. Her disorder was diagnosed as an unusual hormone problem, and she was placed on birth control pills. She had had the sense, since that time, that she was not a normal woman with a normal body. If she could be pregnant, like the therapist, she would prove that her body was normal. Her belief that her body could not conceive, and her need to prove otherwise, seemed to explain in part her promiscuity. The whole issue of her sexual identity and her right to be a sexual woman was opened by her reaction to the therapist's pregnancy.

Another of V's associations to her dream, "the landlord brought the rent down" had to do with the therapist's lowering of her fee for a limited time prior to her pregnancy. V interpreted this as a sign that she was special, that the therapist would take her in, be her mother, and push the other baby out. From this evolved one of the first in-depth discussions of the maternal transference in both its positive and negative aspects. V spoke of her attachment and shared feelings similar to those she had had when her mother died, specifically in anticipating the therapist's leave and the interruption in treatment. As V verbalized her fears, "if the baby was sick, would you cancel my appointment?" she did what she could never do before or after her mother's death. She could separate, feel, and mourn—breaking a pattern of acting out angry demands that she be allowed to stay a child and that her mother be alive to care for her. She was now able to solidify her gains in creating a more independent and successful life for herself.

SUMMARY

The pregnancy of the therapist is an event that has a considerable impact on the analytic process. It is a public event that becomes an ongoing reality in the treatment as it disrupts the formerly consistent, empathic setting and makes impossible a neutral, nonintrusive, all available therapist. It is an event that echoes a wide range of response. While often difficult and at times intimidating for both therapist and patient, the recognition and analytic understanding of the patient's response is an invaluable avenue to therapeutic gains. It heightens the focus on the transference and the real relationship and calls upon the resources of the working alliance between patient and therapist. The result is that the patient and therapist share an event beyond the usual frame of treatment. Their willingness to make it their mutual history is the basis for therapeutic empathy, repair, and growth.

CHAPTER 4

Countertransference Reactions During The Therapist's Pregnancy

Consideration of the therapist's countertransference becomes critical during the therapist's pregnancy. This chapter offers a comprehensive examination—both theoretically and clinically—of this element of the treatment process as it emerges and is experienced over the course of the therapist's pregnancy. Countertransference is defined here in terms of two factors: (1) therapist responses (behaviors, impulses, images, and defense mechanisms, etc.) that stem specifically from her own issues, conflicts, and history, termed, "countertransference predisposition" (Racker, 1968); and (2) therapist responses specifically made in reaction to the patient and the analytic situation (Racker, 1968; Greenson, 1972; Gunther, 1976).

Pregnancy is divided into trimesters, each a period of three months or, more precisely, thirteen weeks, within which there are well-defined stages of development. The first trimester dates from the conception, or rather the awareness of the pregnancy, to the quickening, or perception of fetal movement, usually in the beginning of the fourth month. The second trimester, which is usually the calmest, dates from the beginning of the fourth month to the end of the sixth month. The final trimester dates from the end of the sixth month to the beginning of labor and delivery of the child.

As soon as she is aware of being pregnant, a woman is confronted with a number of issues involving self-image, integration of roles, maternal identification, awareness and exposure of sexuality, and reassessment and redefinition of the male–female relationship (Ballou, 1978). She must face the question of who she is and whether she can maintain a sense of self while making an investment in another who will be an integral part of herself. She must come to grips with her changing body image and her new physical and emotional vulnerability. She must redefine old roles and integrate new ones without a sense of panic or narcissistic loss. She must integrate her "maternal ego ideal" (Turrini, 1980, p. 137) with the reality of her experience with her own mother and resolve some issues of dependence and independence. She must negotiate a position of becoming a mother without experiencing guilt or anxiety for usurping her own mother's place. She must reconcile parental introjects with the visible proof of her sexual relationship with a man. Finally, she must shift from the dyadic relationship with a man to a triadic unit that includes a baby (Breen, 1975).

These issues are significantly compounded for the pregnant therapist. In terms of her self-image, a pregnancy must at first present an emotional and technical quandary. Generally, a therapist's image of herself is characterized by a professional, emotionally muted, somewhat anonymous stance (Greenson, 1972). Certainly the spontaneous, "real" person of the therapist does show at times, but it is generally not the position one is encouraged or trained to take. The obvious nature of a pregnancy, however, makes anonymity and neutrality impossible. The therapist is exposing a very real, very significant life event. Accordingly, she must negotiate a new image of herself, one that allows for disclosure and that can accommodate a human, changing, at times vulnerable, less than idealized view of self.

Anxiety is associated not only with the integration of this new image, but also with the anticipation of patients' responses to it. Like other countertransference reactions, the therapist's anxieties are often "complemented" by the patient's. One male patient, for example, on finding out that his therapist was pregnant, responded, "You can't be pregnant. Doctors don't get pregnant. Nurses get pregnant." The fact is that the therapist had been wrestling with that same myth!

In terms of her sexuality, the therapist must understand not only her own conflicts and history, but also the fact that pregnancy is a disclosure of sexual activity and the relationship with a man. The consistently reported tendency of male patients to fail to recognize the therapist's pregnancy in the early months and to avoid directly dealing with it once known (Lax, 1969; Fenster, 1983) may be a function of the therapist's countertransference. This delay in response may actually reflect the therapist's discomfort and the projected disapproval and withdrawal she anticipates from males.

The identification and integration of a mothering role with one's role as therapist is a complex one to negotiate. On a practical level, there are few cultural or professional models for this dual role. Although women in all professions have moved toward integration of mothering with career, there is still considerable anxiety surrounding it. Part of their anxiety may involve reconciling a dual role with the position of one's own mother, whose primary role was often that of child-caretaker. For the professional woman to do something different, even if there are guidelines, may threaten an idealization of her mother, her childhood, and in some ways herself. Dynamically, the transference pull by patients, and the countertransference response, to be the idealized mother, exists at times for all therapists. For the pregnant therapist, the pull may be intensified. Accordingly, she must be very aware of her own need to mother, and it is crucial that she understand where her issues end and the patient's begin. Whereas in her personal life she must blend family and career roles, as therapist she must be able to differentiate her personal and professional "mothering."

The difficulty of integrating dual roles while reconciling the countertransference aspects is reflected in the therapist's need to be the all-available, idealized mother. This arouses anxiety in the therapist as she inevitably realizes that she cannot be all available to patients and all available to her future child. It creates a countertransference position that makes her vulnerable to those patients (usually narcissistic or borderline) who need an idealized parent and respond to any dimension of the treatment with a feeling of deprivation, betrayal, or rage. Although able to explore the patient's response, the therapist often finds that she is left feeling guilty, then angry. Her guilt may be understood in terms of Racker's (1968) notion of complementary countertransference, that is, the therapist's own needs have caused her to identify with the patient's idealized introject, incorporate the patient's expectations, and experience guilt and anger for being unable to fulfill them.

THE FIRST TRIMESTER

Characteristically the first trimester is a time of strong mixed emotions—excitement and joy in the anticipation of a child coupled with anxiety and fear. Because there is, as yet, no overt manifestation of a baby, fears and anxieties surrounding the baby's well being are heightened. Such fears are often exacerbated by the general physical fatigue, nausea, and discomfort of the initial trimester as well as by the inability of the outside world automatically to validate the pregnancy. Thus, the first trimester is generally a time of self-absorption and concern for self and the baby. In a sense, the increased attention to self prepares the pregnant woman for the vast expenditure of energy needed for maternal functioning.

The countertransference anxieties associated with the issues of the first trimester might be considered both "depressive" and "paranoid" (Racker, 1968). These feelings involve not only the fear that in some way the pregnancy will harm or otherwise negatively affect the patient and his or her treatment, but the fear that anger will be directed at the therapist because of her pregnancy and negatively affect her and her baby. The impact of this anxiety, and the attempt to deal with it, adds to the self-absorption and distraction experienced by the pregnant therapist during the first trimester.

Adding to the self-absorption and distance often experienced by the therapist at this time is the feeling of "carrying" a secret. The authors' position of allowing patients to recognize and ask about the pregnancy at their own pace serves the patient's emotional readiness, but interferes with the therapist's attempted neutrality. The experience of having a hidden agenda contributes to feelings of uneasiness and fears of not being objective. It physically confronts the pregnant therapist with the limits of her empathy, a reality for any therapist in any treatment, but one that becomes poignant for the pregnant therapist, particularly as she works with those struggling with infertility, pregnancy, abortion, or related issues.

THE SECOND TRIMESTER

The second trimester is generally considered the most peaceful time of the pregnancy, with the fewest complications. During these months most women experience "the quickening," which both confirms the pregnancy and relieves some of the fear of losing the child. The visibility of the pregnancy at this stage also underscores its reality as it allows for validation and support by the outside world.

An examination of the countertransference position during the second trimester reveals less anxiety, increased empathy, selective disclosure, awareness by the therapist of patients' responses to the pregnancy and increased interest in and understanding of varied reactions of patients. Because there tends to be a reduction in the anxiety of the therapist, perhaps due to fewer physical discomforts in the second trimester, the therapist often can relax and allow the pregnancy situation to generate important issues within the treatment process.

Barbanel (1980) maintains that "although the therapist may find herself withdrawing energy from the therapeutic situation to her own body, she also may find that her empathic and intuitive reso-nance with patients is heightened as she becomes more sensitized to her own body" (p. 238). Similarly, one of the authors found that during the second trimester, and continuing into the third trimester, she experienced herself as more empathic with patients. There was a sense of being extremely absorbed with them and very attuned to the transference, with less physical and emotional stress.

The therapist is often better able in the second trimester to create a climate of disclosure with patients, that is, to validate the reality of the pregnancy for patients while at the same time letting them respond to it in a way most appropriate to their own histories and psychic constellations. Once the therapist achieves a certain amount of comfort with patients' awareness of her pregnancy, it becomes possible for her to use the feelings engendered in her to further understand patients' reactions.

In her fourth month of pregnancy, for example, one of the authors had a dream about a particular patient. Although she could not remember the details of the dream, her associated feeling to the dream was one of anxiety. Her associations and thoughts regarding the particular patient revealed that this was a person who had always been very intrusive and who became even more so after the disclosure of the pregnancy. The patient's questions were often so personal that they caught the therapist off guard. The therapist began to see that part of her anxiety regarding this patient was a response to the patient's attempt to resist her rage toward the therapist and the baby for changing their alliance. The patient's defense was an attempt to intrude and merge.

Another patient, who had been trying to have a second child for a number of years, entered treatment when the therapist was about four months pregnant. The therapist's feelings of discomfort and anxiety in the face of this patient's persistent questions about her feelings, weight, plans for child rearing, and the like were essentially a countertransference response to the patient's need to idealize the therapist as a result of the pregnancy. In addition to the therapist's countertransference urge to live up to the patient's idealized expec-tations, her discomfort pertained to her anticipation of the patient's envy.

By the middle of the second trimester it is impossible to consider the transference dynamics of patients who continue to deny the pregnancy without exploring the therapist's countertransference, which tends to be particularly salient with male patients. Like other therapists (Lax, 1969; Fenster, 1983), the authors have found that male patients take considerably longer than female patients to openly recognize the pregnancy. For instance, among one of the authors' male patients, none noted the pregnancy in the first trimester; one noted it in the second trimester; and all other male patients did not take note of it until the seventh or eighth month. In accounting for this circumstance, we call attention to Lax's (1969) hypothesis that male patients, unable to gratify or compensate for pregnancy envy by an identification with the female therapist, tend to suppress and isolate their response. But we believe that countertransference issues also play a role in male patients' difficulty in recognizing and addressing the therapist's pregnancy.

With respect to these latter issues, Racker's (1968) consideration of the "neurotic part," or the therapist's repetition of various aspects of the oedipal situation as part of the "total countertransference," is valuable. The author whose male patients had avoided recognition of her pregnancy had herself experienced considerable anxiety in dealing with these patients. She was more self-conscious about her appearance, more anxious before their sessions, and more fearful of negative reactions. Her anticipation of disapproval by male patients may have been a function of her response to male patients as father figures. Hence, there may have been a need to deny her sexuality, as well as her involvement with another man (husband), by avoiding the topic of the pregnancy. There may have been a subtle collusion with male patients not to see, not to explore, not to understand the disguised association in a dream or the hidden awareness of the pregnancy in a look or comment. It would be difficult for her to respond to a male patient's expression of rejection, disgust, or disappointment about the pregnancy if she was struggling with a fear of losing male (paternal) approval.

The liability of this countertransference position is the difficulty it creates for adequately analyzing the full range of patients' responses. In this case, there was not enough focus on male patients' perceptions of the pregnancy, their envy of the baby, their envy of the therapist's creative abilities, the therapist's relationship with another male figure, and the male patients' feelings of exclusion, deprivation, and humiliation. Evidence that there was an incomplete analysis of this material is reflected in the fact that all three patients who terminated upon the therapist's return from having the baby (no one terminated during the pregnancy) were males. In addition, it may be that the therapist's countertransference feelings of self-consciousness, anxiety, and guilt actually made it impossible for patients to be angry with her. Because there was no room for them to express rage or deprivation or to sort out feelings, they had to terminate.

Whatever the specific issues and conflicts set into motion within the therapist in the course of an analysis, the reality and progression of her pregnancy in the treatment arena heightens the intensity of her response. To this extent, it is crucial for the pregnant therapist to seek to understand her countertransferential position and its impact. ⟩C.T.

According to Racker (1968), every transference situation provokes a countertransference reaction that arises from the therapist's early history, neurotic conflicts, and identification with the patient's internal objects. When patients recognize the pregnancy of their therapist, they respond in ways that are characteristic of their own infantile conflicts and character constellations. These differential reactions prompt varying countertransference responses in the therapist. An example of this follows:

T, a 30 year old female patient, entered twice weekly psychoanalysis because of serious marital problems. Reflecting her fear and defensive style was a denial of the reality of her husband's physical abuse, cocaine addiction, and a consolidation of their marital problems into the battle of her wanting a child and his refusing. Underscoring the level of her denial was the fact that although she was a physician's assistant, she remained unaware and confused about the signs of her husband's blatant cocaine addiction. Consistent with this denial, T, who entered treatment shortly before the therapist became pregnant, failed to make any overt reference to the pregnancy until almost the beginning of the third trimester. Considering the quick recognition of the pregnancy by many female patients (Lax, 1969), and in view of the patient's medical expertise, her lack of response reflects her characterlogical denial of situations generating anxiety and negative feelings like rage, envy, and competition.

This reaction prompted specific countertransference feelings and reactions. Aware of the patient's failure to respond, the therapist colluded in the denial for almost seven months. When opportunities arose to underscore the reality, through dream or associated material, the therapist hesitated because of anxiety about the patient's envy or resentment. On analyzing her own position, the therapist began to see that her caution and tendency to overlook the pregnancy with this patient was a function of her own use of denial in relation to sibling competition. The therapist became aware that in her own family situation she was both competitive with and guilty about her success in certain tasks in comparison with that of an older sister. There was both the need to win and the need to play down success or the prize as a way of relieving guilt at having achieved something that her sister wanted but could not achieve. To grapple with the patient's nonrecognition of the pregnancy would have put the therapist in the position of facing her older sister. Once the therapist could grasp the counter-transference issue, she was better able to respond to the patient's denied awareness and feelings.

THE THIRD TRIMESTER

The final trimester of pregnancy is marked by an increase in self-absorption and a concern with issues of life, death, separation, and attachment. Accordingly, the task of the therapist is compounded by the need to face these issues not only in her personal life but also with her patients and in her relationship with them.

Despite the fatigue and physical discomfort of the last three months, most women develop a "nesting behavior" in readiness for the child. This drive to prepare for the coming child can take the form of wall papering, oven cleaning, floor scrubbing, and so forth. To some extent, a parallel "nesting behavior" may be observed in the analytic situation, taking the form of a drive to provide closure with patients. For example, it became very important for one of the authors to make arrangements for certain more fragile patients to see another therapist during her two month leave. Also, at this time she took efforts to update her records on patients, her listings of their names, numbers, addresses, so that someone else could take care of them if necessary.

Raphael-Leff (1980) suggests that "the fear of death during or following delivery is very common among contemporary women despite the advances in medicine and the infrequency of complications" (p. 189). Although the therapist just mentioned did not consciously experience a fear of death as the time of delivery drew near and was comfortable exploring patients' verbalizations of such fears, some sense of fear was reflected in her need to organize everything about the practice. As she analyzed her feeling, she came to understand that the conscious fear was of not returning as she was, of somehow not being able to do or be there for her patients as she was before the baby. Offerman-Zuckerberg (1980) describes it as a concern for "self-survival," the therapist's concern about her own inner resources, her ability to be both therapist and mother, to survive those kinds of demands (p. 167).

Another issue the therapist must face in the third trimester is separation. One of the realities of the third trimester is that the treatment has become time limited—both therapist and patient live with the awareness that an interruption is inevitable.

In terms of the countertransference anxiety regarding this separation, there is not only the fear of losing patients in the practical sense, but fear of the emotional loss often associated with separating from patients. One author, for example, came to understand her increasing anticipation of loss during the last trimester as losing her definition of self, her identity as a therapist, which had been validated by the presence of her patients. In addition, there was a sense that, unlike a vacation, this separation would be different by reason of the investment she anticipated making in her child. There was concern that this separation would involve some major change in the person and therapist she had been.

It is the authors' experience that during the third trimester the baby becomes an imminent reality and, as Winnicott (1956) suggests, the therapist experiences a "primary maternal preoccupation." She longs for time to tune into self and fantasize about the baby and her mothering role. There is often a need and a desire to split off these fantasies from work with patients. Possibly as a reaction to this, patients during the third trimester tend to tune in again to the reality of the baby, whereas in the second trimester many had moved away from the specific content of the pregnancy to their own issues. Often patients' anxieties about the therapist going into early labor or suddenly not appearing for their sessions take the form of comments, questions and nurturing gestures toward the therapist. The therapist's urge to dismiss such comments or to move quickly away from them may reflect a need to remain self-absorbed, to keep involvement with the baby separate from treatment.

The pregnant therapist must accept the impossiblity of predicting exactly how her treatment with patients will turn out. There is no way to determine precisely how they will experience the interruption, their final reactions, and their own experiences of it. The authors have found that setting a final date in advance for patients is crucial. Whether it be a week before delivery or two months, the prior setting of this date provides a frame within which transference and countertransference issues may emerge. The experience of one of the authors is particularly striking in this regard:

A date had been set for a week before delivery as the last day the therapist would see patients. A week before that date there was more than a coincidental number of crises: a patient who had been fighting the possibility of a divorce had her husband served with papers; a male college student announced that he was planning to take a leave of absence from school; a patient reported that her husband's illness had been diagnosed as terminal; a woman who had an affair over the course of the first few months of the analyst's pregnancy announced that she had told her husband of the affair, allowed her husband to meet her lover, and was panicked and unable to function; a supervisee reported feeling that she was in crisis and that she would no longer be able to handle sexual material with a new patient.

Apart from conceptualizing her patients' dynamics, the therapist's response was to wonder if on some level she was triggering the crises. She became aware that at the time of these crises she had been worrying about being without her patients while at the same time she was struggling to provide a sense of closure. She had, in fact, dreamed that she was a day camp counselor with a busload of handicapped children and that she could not take care of her group any longer. In the dream she searched for another counselor to take care of these children.

When considering this, it became apparent to the therapist that she was struggling with a need somehow to take care of or close up all the problems of her patients before leaving. Their crises were, among other things, an attempt to stay connected to the therapist and prevent closure. Another possible interpretation of their crises was as a response to the therapist's verbal and nonverbal cues that they should have their crises while she was still there to respond.

Whether the therapist shares the information about the child's birth with her patients, and when and how she makes this disclosure, is a very subjective decision. It is a function of who she is as therapist and person and how she feels. What is crucial, regardless of her position, is her recognition of the impact on patients and on the treatment process long after she has returned from her leave.

In summary, the countertransference issues of the pregnant therapist are powerful and complex. Here, as with other significant public events in a therapist's life, the therapist has the opportunity to be strikingly aware of her part in the analytic process. If she can confront herself in these countertransference issues, the growth for both self and patient is invaluable.

CHAPTER 5

Alterations in the Treatment Process: Implications for Technique

Throughout this volume, we consider the impact of the therapist's pregnancy on the analytic process, on the patient, and on the therapist herself. Integral to all three aspects of treatment are the subtle—and often unconscious—changes that the analyst assumes in her style and technique over the course of her pregnancy. As a result of physiology, emotional factors, and the presence of a time-limited, shared event in the consultation room, the analyst may approach interactions, problems, or unconscious material in a different way. Some changes may be demanded by, and appropriate to, the modifications the pregnancy introduces into the psychoanalytic frame; others may reflect underlying countertransference difficulties. This chapter examines modifications in the treatment process from two perspectives: first, changes that the authors believe are necessary for the adequate exploration of the impact of the pregnancy; second, changes that occur spontaneously. These changes will be discussed against the backdrop of previous writings on the subject of alterations in the clinical setting and technique.

THE SETTING

The therapeutic situation provides an atmosphere and a setting, a context within which symbolic communication may develop. The therapeutic situation is a reflection of the analyst's role and technique. It offers the patient an implicit statement about the analyst's intent and function: ". . . to listen to (the patient), to concern himself with him without requiring the patient to be concerned with (the analyst), and to protect the contact between them from external interruptions or distraction" (Rycroft, 1968, p. 64).

This setting provides an environment of consistency and security which patients come to expect and on which they rely: the appointment time, the fixed length of sessions, and fee; the analyst's person, role, and consistency of approach; the analyst's *relative* anonymity; and the exclusive one-to-one relationship (Langs, 1975). The reliability of these elements creates a therapeutic "holding environment" (Winnicott, 1963) within which the process of analysis may flourish.

When the analyst becomes pregnant, many of these assumptions about the therapeutic setting are altered. The pregnancy modifies this holding environment on many levels. A concrete, irreversible, and evocative stimulus has been introduced—by the analyst herself—into the relative insularity of the consulting room and therapeutic dyad.

The one-to-one relationship is modified; the analyst–patient dyad has been transformed by the reality of the pregnancy, a potential third person. Many patients allude to the presence of a phantom "third party" (the baby); their relationship with the analyst no longer feels quite as exclusive. For example, one therapist in Fenster's study (1983) described two female patients who became angry "because they couldn't talk about themselves, they had to be concerned with (the therapist) in the sessions. The baby had been an intruder . . . ever since they found out (she) was pregnant" (p. 54).

Another assumption of the setting is the analyst's relative anonymity. This is also confronted during her pregnancy. The patient now becomes tantalized by suggestive glimpses into the analyst's existence in, and relationship to, the outside world. Patients may become aware, perhaps for the first time, of the analyst's reality as a separate person. That the analyst is a sexual person, with intimate relationships of her own, also becomes undeniable. More important, the analyst's physical self changes before the patient's very eyes. The analyst's internal processes may be screened from some patients only with extraordinary effort. The analyst may feel elated or physically drained, for example. But even barely noticeable changes can cue the patient—the analyst may sit differently, the timing or character of her interventions may change, she may become more active or passive, her responsiveness may be compromised or enhanced by shifts in mood or sensitivity. As a result, the patient may be drawn into pondering the analyst—who she is, what she is experiencing, how her pregnancy is affecting their work together. A most basic aspect of the analytic situation is called into question—the analyst's visible stability as a person, the ". . . clear, tangible, durable, unambiguous form of ourselves . . ." (Nacht, 1958, p. 236). Thus, the analyst may no longer seem like quite the same person. As a result, the patient's sense of security may be disrupted.

Borderline and narcissistic patients in particular (Berman, 1975; Fenster, 1983; Lax, 1969), often react directly to the introduction of shifts, however subtle. Such comments as "You are supposed to always be the same" or "You didn't tell me you were going to get pregnant," typify the ways patients experience this break in consistency and security.

Bleger (1967) and Langs (1975) maintain that any disruption in the consistency of the therapeutic setting will precipitate a catastrophic situation. This catastrophe occurs because the stability of the setting—its ground rules and boundaries—is equated unconsciously with the most primitive aspect of the developing self. These aspects of the nascent self have a strong basis in the early symbiosis between mother and child. The frame is equated with the symbiotic elements of the patient–analyst relationship. Hence, a break in its consistency is experienced by the patient as a failure of the earliest, holding aspects of the mother–child dyad.

Eissler (1953) believes that even minor changes in the analyst's technique, an important aspect of the setting, risk changing the character of the psychoanalytic process, leaving essential resistances unanalyzed. Eissler termed such deviations in analytic technique "parameters" and called for their use only in special cases, when the patient's pathology was unmodifiable using interpretation alone. In addition, he recommended that the use of a parameter should eventually lead to its self-elimination.

Thus, the pregnancy of the analyst confronts the therapeutic process with inevitable departures in the setting, which necessitate corresponding modifications in the analyst's technique. When changes in technique are well chosen and understood, they can both preserve the analysis and expand its context. We consider that such unavoidable events and modifications in setting do, in fact, enrich the analytic process; for example, there is an intensification of the transference with a corresponding change in perceptions of the analyst as a real person. It is the recognition and understanding of such alterations, rather than the need to repudiate them, that becomes central to the integrity of the analysis.

TECHNIQUE

From the moment of recognition of the pregnancy, virtually all communication from the patient must be seen as potentially reflective of the meaning of the pregnancy and the breach in the setting. As the analysis becomes suffused, directly or indirectly, with the emotional reverberations of the pregnancy, the patient seeks to cope with, repair, deny, rage against, or withdraw from this breach, this new experience with the analyst.

From the perspective of technique, a change in focus becomes inevitable in order to adequately address these phenomena. The analyst's usual free-floating attention must give way to an alertness to the seemingly disparate disconnected associations, and implicit or explicit allusions to the pregnancy. This therapeutic discipline of considering all conscious and unconscious material as potential vicissitudes of this event serves to validate reality, prevent split-off responding, confront acting out, and highlight the analysis of transference. Such a focus provides the treatment with a defined lens through which the analyst may clearly observe and integrate the patient's experience at this time.

SPECIAL EVENT DYNAMICS

To understand these changes in setting and in the analyst's technique, the dynamics of special events in the life of the therapy is pertinent. As described earlier (Chapter One) in this volume a special event is defined as "anything which alters or intrudes upon the basic analytic situation" (Weiss, 1975, p. 75). Such events include chance meetings between analyst and patient, the analyst's illness and the like. The occurrence of a special event seems to heighten the contrast between the analyst as a real person and as a transference figure (Tarnower, 1966; Weiss, 1975; Katz, 1978).

Therapeutic handling of the special event should involve a recognition of and attentiveness to the event itself, an invitation to free association with respect to it, an attempt to understand the genetic connections that determine the patient's particular reactions, and an acknowledgment that something special and different has, in fact, occurred. Central to these technical foci is the underlying assumption that a special event directly and intensively effects transference feelings. According to Weiss (1975), failure to recognize the impact of the special event on the transference can result in technical errors that may jeopardize an entire treatment.

Interviews with pregnant therapists (Fenster, 1983) corroborate this conclusion. A majority of the therapists felt that the pregnancy itself had furnished the treatment with a vehicle for heightening the transference and mobilizing its expression. Intense anxieties regarding the therapist's unavailability, for example, readily led to discussions of the availability of important people in patients' own lives. Such feelings often spurred the revelation of previously unspoken memories or new historical material.

Also reported by the therapists in Fenster's study was the mobilization of patients' expressions of caring and attachment toward their therapist. There was a new awareness of needing the therapist or the therapist's important place in their lives. Many of these patients had previously defended themselves against any awareness of such an attachment. Thus, the pregnancy was the vehicle for new feelings of closeness within the treatment.

Weiss (1975) had discussed the technical errors that may occur as a result of the intrusion of the special event into the treatment situation. Such errors occur most vividly in the arena of the transference. He cites the wish of both patients and analysts to return to the "safety and regression of the analytic situation and to the silent gratification of the transference" (p. 75). In the face of the special event of the therapist's pregnancy, such wishes may be particularly powerful. Unlike the isolated special event, the pregnancy forces both analyst and patient, over a period of months, to deal with a powerful, *ongoing*, undercurrent in the treatment. As a result, there may be a collusion between client and analyst to act as if the analytic relationship can remain a dyad, untouched by the real presence of the baby-to-be.

Recognizing this possibly denied, but critical, impact on the transference, the pregnant analyst must actively pursue—through interpretations and questions—the significance and meaning of the pregnancy and the breach in the setting for the patient. These interpretations should allude to the feelings of disruption, betrayal, shock, and anxiety that often stem from the change in the therapist. Even if these feelings are not overtly stated or visible, they are assuredly there.

INTERVENTIONS

Consistent with this pursuit of transference feelings is the overall increase in verbal activity on the part of the analyst. The pregnant analyst tends to question, confront, clarify, acknowledge, and interpret more than usual (Fenster, 1983).

This heightened verbal activity is probably due to at least two factors. First, as noted, the therapist's pregnancy often evokes new feelings, thoughts, dream material, and fantasies pertinent to the relationship. More important, in some patients the pregnancy may stimulate acting out. Indeed, many writers have noted more acting out, including lateness or cancellations, during the pregnancy (Lax, 1969 Berman, 1975; Fenster, 1983;). This acting out requires more energetic questioning, confrontation, and interpretation than is usual, since the continuation of these behaviors could prove destructive to the treatment itself.

In particular, the analyst may need to make what Bellak and Faithorn (1981) call a "cathartic interpretation." The therapist here points out elements of the patient's experience that are still unconscious, without waiting for all the derivative material that ordinarily paves the way for an interpretation. If the analyst can understand as quickly as possible the meaning of the patient's acting out and formulate it by relating the contemporary acting out to childhood events or preconscious needs, the resulting interpretations will often prove cathartic, triggering the verbalization of previously unconscious, unverbalized feelings, ideas or conflicts. Consequently, acting out can often be curtailed.

If acting out or intense anxiety are understood as a response to the therapist's empathic failure (by virtue of her "insensitivity" in becoming pregnant), immediate interpretation may help the patient understand how he or she is responding and why. Through this process, the empathic link is restored. The patient has been able to live through a potentially disintegrating or angering experience without, it is hoped, catastrophe and with the sense that breaches are not irrevocable.

The following case illustrates the therapeutic use of a cathartic interpretation:

> N, a 46-year-old woman with three children, was in twice weekly analysis for two years at the time of the analyst's pregnancy. She recognized the pregnancy early through several dreams in which doctors were preoccupied and not adequately attending to her treatment. She began to come late to sessions and miss some completely. Following one missed session, N angrily accused the analyst of forgetting about her (N's) children's needs because of preoccupation with the analyst's own self and child-to-be. The analyst at this point interpreted N's terror of losing the analyst as a caretaker, as N felt she had lost her own mother with the birth of her younger brother. Not only had N lost the mother's care, but she also had had to relinquish her own childhood to care for her brother when her mother became depressed following the birth. The patient's missed sessions were expressions of her anxiety, her fear of having to take care of the analyst (who might become depressed), and her rage. She wanted a return of her rights to be a child-patient. After these feelings were interpreted, N spoke quite emotionally of her feelings of abandonment and terror at

having to become an adult while still a child. These feelings were directly connected with her own difficulties in mothering her three children. She subsequently came regularly to her appointments.

Another significant factor affecting the analyst's change in technique, particularly her tendency to intervene more actively, is the sense of pressure as time passes and the break in treatment draws near. This time constraint imposed by the pregnancy frequently prompts analytic work akin to that done during a termination (Fenster, 1983). As the sense of time passing becomes more acute, the therapist becomes more active, perhaps feeling pressed to "complete" work that will shortly be interrupted. The therapist and patient may feel a need to review the treatment to date. Some patients become fearful of—or actually experience—a return of earlier symptoms. There may be intense resistance to a discussion of underlying feelings about the pregnancy or, alternatively, total preoccupation with the event and its ramifications.

Reassurance from the therapist that she plans to return is critical, as are discussions regarding the patient's fears about the therapist's not returning, her unavailability, and so forth. The therapist's increased level of intervention is overdetermined, being a response to the upsurge of new material, the patient's acting out, and the press of time. It is our strong conviction that such an active response not only is warranted, but is crucial to the integrity of the analytic work at this time. This more active stance, occurs, of course, within the framework of analysis. There must be a constant effort to explore with patients the meaning and the relation to the past and present of their responses to the pregnancy. In this way, even while changes do occur, the analytic attitude of the therapist remains constant.

THE REAL RELATIONSHIP AND SELF-DISCLOSURE

The analyst's pregnancy forcefully confronts the patient with the real aspects of the analyst as a person. All patients, whether consciously or unconsciously, will speculate at one time or another about their analyst. What she wears, how her office is decorated, how her interventions address the issues—all suggest the analyst's tastes, values, points of view. Stone (1961) has written cogently about this kind of implicit communication from therapist to patient about therapist.

Such information about the analyst has been found by many writers to contribute to an essential aspect of the treatment—the total, human relationship with the analyst. Greenson and Wexler (1969) state that addressing the patient's reactions to the "real" analyst strengthens the therapeutic alliance and facilitates "the acceptance of transference interpretations when made" (p. 34). Greenson (1971; Greenson and Wexler, 1969) conceptualized the real relationship between patient and analyst as a legitimate and necessary aspect of the analytic situation. Greenson and Wexler (1969) write that

> to facilitate the full flowering and ultimate resolution of the patient's transference reactions, it is essential in all cases to recognize, acknowledge, clarify, differentiate, and even nurture the non-transference or relatively transference-free reactions between patient and analyst. This may require non-interpretive or non-analytic interventions, but these approaches are vastly different from anti-analytic procedures [p. 361].

Little (1951) feels that it is part of the analyst's task to bring the patient's perceptions of the "actual and psychic" truth about the analyst to light. Such real, or nontransferential aspects of the therapeutic relationship are, according to Nacht (1958), crucial to the eventual resolution of the transference. Thus, those authors assert that the therapist's human, straightforward, genuine, and realistic interactions with the patient can contribute to the patient's ultimate willingness to accept and examine underlying transference and resistance feelings.

Because the therapist's pregnancy enters so directly into the treatment as an unavoidable aspect of the therapist herself, it provides fertile ground for a consideration of the real relationship. In Fenster's (1983) study, participants judged themselves to be significantly more self-revealing than usual with their patients during the pregnancy. In addition, many of these therapists reported resisting the wish to be even more self-disclosing.

This internal and external push towards self-disclosure serves a critical function in the real relationship. It is an acknowledgment that the pregnancy is indeed an event shared by patient and analyst. It expresses a recognition that the patient is a part of the process of the pregnancy and may realistically need to have certain information about the analyst's experience. It is an expression of the analyst's own pleasure in her pregnancy and the experience of having a baby—an important role-modeling function for many patients who grapple with ambivalence about having children. In the sharing of this most basic human experience, the genuine connection between therapist and patient can be a bond enhancing patients' ability to tolerate the new tension in the analytic work.

Such nonanalytic interventions reflect an altered or new interactional process that results from the pregnancy. More often than is usual, patients begin to voice fantasies or ask questions of the therapist. The fact of the pregnancy in the room seems to offer them a sense of license or an avenue for questions they were previously unable to articulate. The therapist appears more human, more real, and patients may thus seem more curious, more interested. The new information also triggers elaborate new fantasies about the therapist. For some, the circumstance may be akin to being at the bedroom door while their parents are making love—there is an excitement and a fascination, an urge to get closer along with a simultaneous terror at the possibility of being allowed in the room.

In her interaction with her patients, the pregnant analyst must address the elements of their ongoing relationship while being vigilant for the unconscious material and the implicit and explicit derivatives of the transference. The therapist's usual practice of exploration rather than immediate response when a question is raised often culminates, during pregnancy, in an eventual exchange of information or feelings (Fenster, 1983). Such responsiveness preserves the analytic process while validating the nontransferential, real feelings prompted by the pregnancy and, for some patients, allows a respectful inclusion, a mutuality that enhances ego growth. One therapist in Fenster's study, for example, described a female patient who was reassured by the new, real information she was receiving about her therapist: "She knew that I had a life outside of being her therapist and she presented that [reality] as making her feel closer to me, more comfortable. [Before this, the patient had feared] that she could be over-involved with me or I with her . . . since in her family the boundaries were [nonexistent]" (p. 106).

The intense involvement of patients in a personal event in the therapist's life may eventuate in a sharply felt loss for them after the baby is born. Indeed, patients may anticipate a sense of loss at having been privy to the therapist's pregnancy, "watching the baby grow" as one therapist put it, and then being unable to share in the outcome of this event. This phenomenon was called "the loss of seeing the baby."

Over the course of the pregnancy, then, a patient may move from a sense of inclusion in the therapist's life to one of exclusion later. On the other hand, most patients will gratefully welcome the return to normalcy that follows the baby's birth—the reinstatement of a therapeutic focus on themselves, a return to the dyad that is the analytic relationship.

This brings us to an important issue regarding technique, namely, how much information is too much? Obviously, this is an issue determined both by the therapist's personality and the clinical needs of the individual patient. We have found that such noninterpretive interventions as responding to questions may increase a patient's capacity to empathize, to test reality, and to separate out transference from real perceptions of the analyst. However, such responses may also serve countertransference needs or patients' needs to resist their own ideas or feelings. For example, the analyst may have a greater need to disclose information than the patient has to hear it. She may emphasize certain aspects of her pregnancy or involve the patient because of her own wishes for gratification or closeness. The patient may respond, consciously or unconsciously, with a sense of having been interrupted, intruded upon, or seduced. The patient may resent the pregnancy and its interference in the analysis or become superficially solicitous while remaining subtly uninvolved in his or her own introspective process. Other patients may, in the service of resistance, bask in the overly gratifying personal relationship with the analyst. An emphasis on the real traits of the analyst may also serve to skirt more potent transference feelings.

A fuller cognizance of one's own countertransference needs, in conjunction with the clinical needs of the individual patient, must serve as one's guide. We recommend an analytic stance of active questioning and exploration of fantasies before the therapist reveals personal information. This position may be altered somewhat with adolescent and child patients, who require a more immediately interactive and personally disclosing approach.

Most important, it must be recognized that the real relationship between patient and analyst does not require continued self-revelation for its development. It is more the fact of the pregnancy, the therapist's continuing recognition and acknowledgment of its impact on herself and her patients (both real and transferential), that fosters the genuine connection between them. Therefore, it is essential that questions about and wishes to discuss the therapist herself be continually assessed for both their resistant and their nonresistant components.

SUMMARY

The pregnancy of the analyst is a major event in the life of both analyst and patient. Some patients show little effect, some welcome the opportunity to get to know the analyst as a real person; others become suicidal or precipitate major crises in the management of their own lives. In this chapter, the analyst's pregnancy has been conceptualized as an intrusion by the analyst herself into the good-enough analytic setting, the usual and unarticulated constants that constitute the analytic space. Hence, a sensitive exploration of the meaning of the disruption in the "holding," dyadic nature of the therapeutic settings—as well as the patient's reactions and derivatives related to the meaning of the pregnancy—is essential. In addition, maintenance of the usual therapeutic stance will reassure the patient that the therapist can sustain or restore the holding aspects of the setting despite this temporary, but ongoing, impingement on the relationship.

The intrusion of the pregnancy offers both therapist and patient an unusual, evocative, and reparative moment within the treatment, a chance to meet each other more simply and directly, a moment that holds out the possibility of mutual caring and concern. This positive, interactive aspect of the pregnancy adds a crucial dimension to the element of intrusion and cannot be overemphasized.

Finally, "only analyzing or only interpreting transference phenomena" (Greenson and Wexler, 1969, p. 27) is a therapeutic stance that avoids the patient's integrative, adaptive, and realistic perceptions of the analyst at a time when these perceptions are both prominent and pertinent. By the same token, a stance of continuous factual disclosure, to the exclusion of analytic investigation, will prove ultimately unproductive. Analytic technique which allows for an honest assessment of reality and unreality, especially regarding the therapist herself, is critical to the ongoing working alliance, to the patient's receptivity to interpretation, and to his or her ultimate integration of the reality of the analyst as a person.

Management of Practical Issues

When the therapist confirms that she is pregnant, the stage is set for profound changes in her private and professional life. Side by side with the necessity for a dynamic understanding of the impact of the pregnancy is the need to make many decisions concerning the management of the practice. In this chapter, practical matters are discussed.

It is crucial to realize that the therapist's vision of herself will fluctuate during her pregnancy; hence, she will feel differently about her decisions at different times. The hallmark feeling is conflict— conflict between proving herself a reliable professional versus a good mother.

Initially, the therapist may feel she can conduct business as usual, denying the implications of her pregnancy, her increased physical and emotional vulnerability, and the consequent limitations in her capacity for work. Although the therapist need not be a slave to her physical condition, she has to respect it. She must be realistic and make allowances for her special needs without feeling that this makes her an inadequate therapist.

RECOGNITION

When and how to tell patients about one's pregnancy is usually the first concern. This decision is tied to when the therapist plans to stop working, how long the maternity leave will be, and if she is in fact, returning to work after the baby is born. The authors have found that it is more useful to wait either for the patient to bring up the pregnancy or until derivatives or acting out behavior make it apparent that the issue has been attended to, albeit unconsciously. However, if such derivatives are not forthcoming, it is incumbent upon the therapist to address the fact of her pregnancy directly within a time frame that allows for adequate therapeutic exploration. In our experience and in Fenster's research, we have found that it is never appropriate to let the patient go on indefinitely without bringing the pregnancy into discussion. To do so is clearly acting out on the therapist's part.

The advantage to waiting for patients to display signs of recognition is, first, that waiting gives the patients some degree of control over their psychological readiness to deal with the pregnancy. Additionally, the therapist gains an understanding of how they may continue to react during the pregnancy. Patients who act out awareness will often continue acting out during the course of the pregnancy. This is true for other recognition styles as well. Derivatives (more fully explicated in the chapter on patients' reactions) may include dreams in which the therapist or therapist's representations are seen to be preoccupied, perhaps taking care of someone else besides the patient, dreams of having babies, dreams of mothers, siblings or dreams of the therapist with her children.

In some cases the patient's acting out behavior becomes an indication of unconsciously dealing with the pregnancy. This may take the form of missed sessions, increased resistance, late payments, sexual promiscuity, and concern with dieting. Faced with this behavior, the therapist must work to bring the pregnancy into the conscious arena. Such questions as "Do you think there is any particular reason that you dream more frequently of your mother at this time?" or "Do you think missing sessions a lot lately has to do with something happening in the therapy?" or "I wonder if your desire to have children right now is related to something about me?" may be useful in eliciting the patient's awareness.

Benedek (1973), who was working in a residential treatment center for emotionally disturbed children, has recommended a different approach. In this setting she advised telling both patients and staff immediately, since word travels quickly. Both staff and patients need the opportunity to work through the reality and implications of this event. In a hospital setting, immediately announcing one's pregnancy may be more advantageous than waiting for patient or staff recognition.

Waiting till patients notice the pregnancy can, of course, reach an extreme where the patient never spontaneously notices or verbalizes derivatives indicative of noticing. This is not uncommon. It is therefore necessary to set cut off dates by which time all one's patients have to know. In this way, a patient's denial of and reaction to the therapist's pregnancy and the impending interruption of treatment may be worked with more actively. For the patients who have not mentioned the pregnancy, the ensuing discussion is always revealing of their character, style and dynamics.

The authors are of the opinion that patients should have at least three months prior to the time the therapist plans to stop working to grapple with the issue of the pregnancy openly. It is not easy for many patients to reveal their more negative, unhappy, or envious feelings. There is much cultural pressure for a positive response to pregnancy, and there is the cultural injunction to treat pregnant women with kid gloves. It takes some time to get past the social role playing to more "unacceptable" feelings.

NEW REFERRALS

It is the authors' belief that, from the outset, it is essential for the therapist to tell prospective patients of the pregnancy and the eventual interruption in treatment. If patient and therapist feel this is a workable arrangement, treatment can begin. Some therapists may choose not to take any referrals at this time, particularly those planning to take a maternity leave of over three months.

The authors found that not telling new patients about their pregnancy, either before treatment was started or as soon as the therapist knew, was very disruptive for these patients. It seems as if, not having had the opportunity for an alliance with the therapist before the pregnancy, new patients feel particularly betrayed and overlooked. Transferentially, they seem to have no frame for expanding the perception of the therapist; rather, their initial experience of the therapist is of deprivation and imminent disruption. Fenster (1983) found that new patients were reported as being more resentful than other patients that a secret had been withheld from them. They resented not having had the opportunity of choosing to be in such a relationship. It seems that without the backup of an existing working alliance, feelings of mistrust are more easily engendered.

The therapist may want to consider carefully whom she does take on as a new patient. Excessively hostile, suicidal, extremely dependent, or borderline patients may be inappropriate to take on at this point and are best referred to colleagues. The therapist's increased emotional and physical vulnerability may make these patients' demands or crises difficult to manage. In their own best interests, these patients should be referred to someone who can take on their demands. Fenster (1983) found that pregnant therapists who were working with such "difficult patients" often felt a strong urge to "be rid of" them. When such patients abruptly terminated treatment upon learning of the therapist's pregnancy, only a few of the therapists actively pursued the patient. Other therapists felt that their own self-preoccupation and vulnerability played into an inclination to let these patients go, with a sense of relief.

Although transference reactions may not be resolved during this time period, vigorous and aggressive interpretation is called for to bring the issues to some level of awareness. In this way, the patient can, during the interruption of treatment, perhaps use what has been discussed. Further resolution of pregnancy-related transference issues continues after the therapist returns to work.

THE PERIOD OF INTERRUPTION

If the therapist is not planning to return to work, it is important that she tell her patients about the pregnancy as soon as she has made the decision to terminate. In Fenster's study (1983), this issue most often came up in a job situation rather than in private practice. The issue then becomes one where termination of treatment, with the reactions attendant to ending and not just pregnancy, are considered and worked through. Referral to other therapists privately or within an agency can then be pursued.

When to stop working? At first, the therapist may believe that she can work virtually until labor begins. Fenster (1983) found that there were many therapists who had not set an interruption date and who in retrospect felt they should have done so. It has been the authors' experience that it is preferable and necessary to plan an interruption date with patients. This allows the therapist some conflict-free time to care for herself and prepare for the baby. For all concerned, a preset date will usually relieve the anxious fear that the "water may break" or labor begin during a therapy session. Most importantly, it provides closure and control for all, underlining the reality of the pregnancy and birth. By providing a frame, a preset date engenders work regarding the interruption or termination. It allows for a focus on separation, abandonment, dependency issues, and the like. To fail to set a date is to collude in the denial that the therapist is pregnant and to encourage the misbelief that there will be no interruption and no baby.

The decision about the length of the maternity leave is a personal one. Some therapists feel that they want to go back immediately, and some feel that they never want to go back. The issue is made more

difficult because tentative decisions need to be made early in pregnancy, when the therapist has no idea, especially in the first pregnancy, how she may feel after giving birth. A majority of the
therapists interviewed by Fenster (1983) took off between five and
eight weeks; a small percentage took off a longer period of time. In
retrospect, many of those who returned early said they would have
stayed out longer if they had been able to anticipate how much they
would feel attached to their babies in the first three months postpartum and their own consequent reluctance to return to work. Concern
for oneself, one's baby, and one's patients must be juggled at this
time.

Another issue in the length of a pregnancy leave is how long a
separation patients can emotionally manage and whether they will
feel a strong enough connection to return when the therapist does.
One author, after her first pregnancy, found that with a two-month
leave, all her patients returned fairly easily. With her second child,
she took a three-month postpartum leave, and, again, most patients
returned.

Another author, who was expecting twins, took off a total of seven
months—two months prior to delivery and five after. Of seventeen
patients, three came back when she returned; and of these three only
one remained in treatment. Clearly, a leave of seven months is
tantamount to terminating a practice. In retrospect, it would have
been wise for all concerned to consider this leave a form of termination and to refer patients elsewhere for continued treatment. In
maintaining the illusion of a leave, patients found the separation
very difficult but felt bound to the therapist and were not able to take
appropriate steps toward getting other help. There was a great deal of
acting out of dependency and anger, and only much later, after a year
or two, were some of these patients able to get back into psychotherapy with new therapists.

Both therapist and patient need to state clearly and know the
possibilities and plan for the interruption and return to treatment. It
is important that patients know the approximate date of the therapist's planned return to work, barring any complications. Although
logistics may vary, one possibility is for patients to be told to expect
a letter or call one month prior to the therapist's return. The letter
can contain an appointment date for an initial return appointment,
at which time a regular schedule may be set up. If the initial
appointment time is impossible, patients can be urged to call to
reschedule. The authors found this method to be very effective and
clear, with the letter serving in addition as a transitional connection
to the therapist for the patient.

As further preparation for the inevitable interruption of treatment, referrals to other colleagues during the interim may be considered with patients. Many patients are reluctant to see anyone else, and in most situations it is not necessary. Referrals for continuous treatment, however, need to be considered with patients who are crisis prone or when the therapist's leave is an extended one. In these situations, the first step is to contact colleagues who might be willing to take the referrals. The patient may then be encouraged to make contact with this colleague and even make an appointment before the interruption in treatment. This provides an opportunity for therapist and patient to consider feelings and issues emerging from the referral—issues such as loyalty, displacement, parental competition, and the like. It will also provide the patient with a resource if a crisis erupts.

Referral to another therapist has ramifications for all: How is the new therapist perceived—as a temporary substitute or as a permanent replacement? Is the new therapist an extension of the current therapeutic relationship or a new connection? Will the patient wish to continue with the colleague after the therapist returns? What are the transference and countertransference implications? To what extent are the issues discussed with the substitute therapist split off from the original treatment? In the light of these questions, it is crucial to examine the influence the referral will have on the original analytic process.

The issue of contact with patients during one's absence has been handled in a variety of ways. Often some contact is therapeutically indicated, especially where a patient's object constancy is threatened by the pregnancy and interruption. Patients are often unsure that you will survive, return, and stay if you do come back. There are two types of contacts to be considered. The first is letting patients known that the therapist is "O.K."—reassuring them that she has survived and will return. The level of this contact can be a letter confirming the return appointment time, a birth announcement, a note telling the patient of the birth, or a call telling the patient of the birth. Each level implies a different degree of interpersonal contact with which the therapist must be comfortable. It is important for the therapist to take into account the impact of any interaction with patients during the interruption.

The second type of patient contact during the interruption has to do with the patient's need to reach the therapist for crises or problems. Fenster (1983) found that 19 out of 22 therapists had phone contact with their patients during the therapist's absence. Eight therapists received calls regarding the baby's birth and therapist's health. Fourteen therapists set up appointments by phone. Five had phone contact because of patients' crises during this time; one therapist had weekly contact calls with patients.

This is a complex issue—how available the therapist makes herself and how much of a boundary she maintains in this period of her life. Sometimes the therapist seems to feel an excess of guilt because she has willingly caused this interruption, and she may offer contact as an effort at reparation.

There will inevitably be some crises during the therapist's leave, and the therapist needs to have a procedure for handling such requests for contact. Some therapists see their patients for emergency sessions. Another alternative is to take emergency calls during the leave and refer the patients to a colleague if the crisis warrants further attention. Sometimes crises may be handled by a simple phone contact. Moreover, patients may call not necessarily because there is a real life crisis, but rather to be reassured of the therapist's availability. A third option is not to take any calls but to give patients the name of a colleague to call in the interim.

It should be stressed that the patient's involvement with a colleague adds a parameter to the treatment alliance. After the patient resumes treatment, it is important to discuss the meaning of another therapist's being able to help the patient. The therapist must also deal with her own feelings about another therapist's being able to adequately meet her patient's needs. Such feelings as guilt, overconcern for her patients, omnipotence, possessiveness, or relief, as well as concern over the possible loss of the patient's fees, may complicate the therapist's feelings about relying on colleagues.

Whatever arrangements are made, some patients will not return when the therapist does. In Fenster's (1983) research, more than half of the therapists reported that at least one patient ended treatment while the therapist was on leave. The therapists believed that these terminations were probably due at least in part to some issue related to the pregnancy.

The issue of contact with the therapist may also arise in another way: Patients may want to visit after the birth of the baby. In response to an unwelcome request to call or visit in the hospital, the therapist can simply state her need to have this private time with baby and family. Some patients may call to see if the therapist is truly all right and some may ask to see the baby or even offer to babysit. Sometimes patients' requests to visit may simply be a wish to reaffirm the continuing existence of the therapist, either in reality or in their own minds. Just as requests in the analysis are handled by attempting to recognize the need behind the request, so should requests to see the baby or visit the analyst be addressed and explored.

GIFTS

A sensitive situation that often develops concerns gifts. Many patients will bring gifts prior to the interruption, send gifts during the hiatus from therapy, or on resumption of treatment. How should this be handled? Fenster (1983) found that in all cases gifts were accepted by the therapist but not without a certain degree of conflict about the appropriateness and discussion with patients regarding the meaning of gifts. It was generally felt, however, that because the baby had been such a major part of the interactional system for so many months, it seemed unfair and confusing to patients to refuse this gesture of good will. Although the therapists in this study and the authors did not usually accept gifts under other circumstances, this particular circumstance seemed to call for different behavior. It was felt that the acceptance of such gifts was reparative in nature, especially because the patients have no choice but to become part of this process in the therapist's life. To do other than accept seems somewhat double-binding. The exploration of the meaning of these gifts may also occur later in the treatment in the context of the continuing discussion of the patient's reaction to the interruption of treatment and his or her concerns about changes in the therapist now that she has a child or more children for whom to care.

PATIENTS' QUESTIONS

One of the shifts that occurs during and after the therapist's pregnancy is that patients may begin asking many personal questions. As a rule, one is trained to deal with questions by exploring and analyzing the motivation and fantasies underlying the question. When the therapist is pregnant, there is a distinct and strong pull to answer patients' questions. Part of this pull stems from a feeling of obligation to share some of the real aspects of one's pregnancy because one has brought this real event into the relationship. There is also a narcissistic wish by the therapist to share her experience and feelings.

Some authors (Barbanel, 1980) believe that deciding how much to tell the patient depends on the patient's developmental level and on whether the patient has siblings or children. Titus-Maxfield and Maxfield (1979) suggest that not answering questions and focusing only on the genetic determinants of the patient's reactions may be a resistance by the therapist to the difficult interpersonal process at hand. Clarkson (1980) emphasizes examining the patient's motivation for a question. She cites a couple she was treating who repeatedly asked her about her fatigue and cautioned her to be careful and not get tired. When she asked why it mattered to them that a woman should not get tired when pregnant, the response was a guilt-ridden story of the wife's exhausting shopping trip the day before her son's delivery and his subsequent birth defects and mental retardation.

Fenster (1983) found a significant trend toward self-disclosure and responsivity to patient's questions in her pregnant sample. Some of those therapists felt, in retrospect, that this enhanced the "real" aspects of the relationship, allowing patients to view them as more human. Others felt that they had responded directly more out of guilt, a feeling of owing it to the patient, and that this had obscured underlying issues. The authors hold with Clarkson's (1980) position of throwing the ball back into the patient's court, at least initially, not because the therapist wants to put it there out of her own resistance, but because it belongs there and the patient wants it there as well.

Dynamically, questions are a meaningful reflection of some aspect of a patient's conscious or unconscious experience. Asking questions is an attempt to air feelings, to obtain clarification or validation of the pregnancy. Questions may also reflect the patient's genuine wish to know the therapist as a person. As patients ask questions like "Do you want a boy or a girl? Are you nauseous? Are your legs swollen? Are you happy to be pregnant?" it is important to explore with them whether they themselves might want or have wanted a boy or a girl. Were they (or their wife or mother) nauseous when pregnant? Was there another pregnancy they had strong feelings about? All interest and concern with the therapist's state will likely disappear as they talk of their own wishes, memories, fantasies, and experiences. Sometimes patients' questions are stimulated by a feeling that they *should* be interested and concerned about the therapist. She has taken center stage. Regardless of their attentiveness to the therapist, most patients want the stage back. The therapist can get lost in discussing "real" issues too much just as easily as she can ignore the importance of the "real" issue in terms of its transference and countertransference implications.

With children and adolescents, it is probably more appropriate to be self-disclosing and responsive to questions. It may be important to be concrete in countering feelings of abandonment and depression. To the teenager who asks "Are you nauseous?" an exploration of fantasies about how pregnancy may injure you or make you sick is warranted. Then the therapist may need to explain the physical changes over the trimesters. Similarly, children may need to know immediately what happens during the course of pregnancy and may need in an early session to know the details of your child care arrangements, so that they can be reassured you will return to take care of them.

An area of self-disclosure that can be helpful is giving patients a brief description of one's proposed plans for combining career and motherhood. The therapist wants to convey a sense that there will be someone reliable caring for the baby while she is at work and that she can concentrate fully on her patients when in the office. For many patients there is also a realistic need for a model of a career woman handling the responsibilities of both home and work. The issue of combining career and motherhood is one that the therapist must continually negotiate.

COLLEAGUES

A final issue to be commented on is the reaction of colleagues to the therapist's pregnancy and the effect it can have on the therapist. One reaction the authors noted quite consistently was an intolerance for the therapist's increased vulnerability and encouragement for her to work far beyond what was realistically manageable for her during the time of her pregnancy. The therapist is particularly vulnerable to this type of pressure. If she herself is uncomfortable with her heightened emotionality and increased personal needs, she may blame herself for what she sees as self-indulgence. She may deny her needs and may even take on more work to prove her capability. If the therapist has counterphobically overworked to the extent that she has diminished her effectiveness, she may feel guilty or depressed when she perceives her failure. It conflicts with an image of herself as having unlimited capacity.

Colleagues may take an unpredictable stance in relation to the pregnant analyst and her work. Their responses may include oversolicitious concern, a demand for overcompensation at times of weakness or need for help, jealousy, envy, identification with and anxiety about the burden the therapist is taking on, fear of neglect of themselves, and hostility. Nadelson et al. (1974) noted, as did the authors, that the faculty of a training institution may encourage an "heroic" attitude in the therapist and provide little support for her needs for flexibility. It is vital for the therapist to hold on to her sense of self and her needs in the face of such varied and often strong reactions.

SUMMARY

The pregnant therapist is faced with a unique set of professional issues and quandaries. She must make many decisions early in her pregnancy, before she clearly understands her needs and feelings. Issues to be decided include when to tell patients about the pregnancy, how to handle new referrals, how long a maternity leave to take, how to handle crises during the leave, and how to deal with colleagues' reactions. We have offered guidelines that we have found useful. Each therapist, however, must consider the issues raised here within her existing therapeutic framework. Handled with forethought and awareness of both patients' and therapist's reactions, these practical matters can be negotiated in a manner that preserves the integrity of the treatment.

CHAPTER 7

Treatment of the Adolescent Girl During the Therapist's Pregnancy

Adolescence, the therapeutic situation, and pregnancy share a common bond—all evoke and involve a process of change and regression. Ultimately, the regression in each is in the service of development and the integration of new and old identifications. This chapter explores the interaction between these regressive—and progressive—processes as the adolescent girl and the pregnant analyst meet in an analytic moment of potential mutuality.

The developmental tasks of adolescence have been outlined and discussed by many writers (e.g., Blos, 1962, 1979; A. Freud, 1958; Jacobson, 1961; Masterson, 1972; Laufer, 1975; Golombek and Garfinkel, 1983). Despite the varied points of reference of these writers, there is surprising agreement among them about the psychological conflicts and developmental changes that confront those in the age group between 13 and 21 years. In summarizing these maturational tasks, four general categories may be delineated: 1) emancipation from one's parents, 2) increasing attachments to one's peers and to one individual, 3) the development of the sense of identity in creative work pursuits, and 4) the alteration in attitudes about one's body and sexuality.

Blos (1979) calls adolescence the second individuation process, the first having been completed toward the end of the third year of life with the attainment of self and object constancy. This second individuation process involves "a heightened vulnerability of the personality organization" (p. 142). There is an increase in narcissistic concerns and an upsurge of drives as a result of genital strivings. The self is in a constant state of flux. For girls, a regressive wish to return to the ministering attentions of the active, preoedipal mother emerges. This regressive pull may manifest itself in such varied behaviors as the girl's passivity or dependency vis-à-vis the mother or, on the other hand, in dramatic efforts to turn away from the mother through "boy-craziness" and heterosexual attachments.

For many adolescents entering therapy, it is often difficulties with this second process of individuation, this pull to regress, that bring them to treatment. Such diverse symptoms as cutting classes, failing grades, fights with parents or peers, promiscuity, pregnancy, drug use, disordered eating patterns, isolation, and depression may derive—at their core—from unresolved dependencies and infantile object ties. The therapist is often called on to ease the adolescent (and sometimes the family as well) first into an ongoing process of talking, listening, meaning-making and boundary-making. Ultimately, there can be movement towards true individuation.

For the adolescent girl, the process of individuation entails paradoxical tasks. While attempts at differentiation from the mother are gaining psychological momentum, the adolescent girl is simultaneously consolidating her identifications with her mother as a woman. This involves an ongoing dialectic between acceptance and repudiation, internalization and rejection, as a massive sifting through of the mother's personality, physical attributes, tastes, values, strengths, and weaknesses takes place. So, also, is there a relentless search for alternative models with which to identify, such as those offered by the media, one's teachers, peers, relatives, neighbors, the mothers of friends, and, of course, one's therapist. Particularly when the therapist is a woman, the adolescent girl's seeking out of models and trying on of roles is even more a primary phenomenon within the treatment situation.

Many writers note this characteristic of the adolescent patient to use the therapist as a source of identification. Golombek and Garfinkel (1983), using Blos' framework for thinking about adolescents' intrapsychic growth, describe the secretiveness with which middle adolescents (15–17 years) take in their therapists and adults in general. Laufer (1964) discusses the adolescent patient's identification with the therapist and incorporation of the therapist's attributes. Blos (1979) suggests that the therapist models new concepts of self. All this is taking place in a context of continuous personality flux and differentiation.

Because of these special characteristics, those treating adolescents advocate adaptations in the standard psychoanalytic technique. For example, Blos (1979) writes that, with certain adolescent patients, the therapist must "declare his stand, make explicit who he is, what he can and cannot do . . ." (p. 308). To simply be an emphatic listener is not enough. Rather, the therapist is encouraged to be firm, stimulating, and knowable. Likewise, Golombek and Garfinkel (1983) state that with early adolescents the therapist must be consistent and unflappable, identifying realities and clarifying limits. With middle adolescents, the therapist must become a responsive sparring partner. "For these patients, the therapist must deviate from the orthodox insight-oriented, nondirective stance so useful with adult patients. He must be willing to share some of his own ideas, beliefs, and values with his patients, recognizing their need for identification" (p. 9). In this way, therapists easily convey to their patients a sense of their own individuality and separateness, as well as a tolerance for differences of opinion and values.

The pregnant therapist is also experiencing her own brand of psychological disequilibrium. Having a child is a major transition period for most women and couples. Such changes as those of role, values, relationships, and physiology are occurring (Benedek, 1956; Breen, 1975; Ballou, 1978; Bibring, Dwyer, Huntington, and Valenstein, 1961; Entwisle & Doering, 1981; Pines, 1972, 1982). Pregnancy is a normal developmental crisis, during which partially resolved conflicts reemerge, leading to new levels of intrapsychic equilibrium and organization (Bibring et al., 1961; Breen, 1975). This is true particularly of a first pregnancy.

Conflicts and resolutions about one's own mother, one's femininity, one's marriage, one's identity as a mother and a professional, and one's child-to-be (Ballou, 1975) all emerge at this time. Many writers place special importance on a woman's changing sense of her own mother during pregnancy. Pines (1982) describes a first pregnancy as a developmental phase in a woman's perpetual separation and individuation from her mother. Benedek (1956) suggests that heightened dependency needs during pregnancy rekindle feelings and memories about the early relationship with one's mother.

Thus, the pregnant therapist, like the adolescent girl, is undergoing many shifts in her sense of herself, her body, her sexuality; her relationship with her own mother, and her identity as a woman. Both therapist and patient are experiencing a process of psychological evolution and physiological change, a transition in their development as women.

It is shocking that considering these phenomena, not one article has been published to date on the adolescent patient in treatment with the pregnant therapist. Two writers have, however, concerned

themselves with the treatment of children. Browning (1974) described increased mechanisms of denial regarding the pregnancy,
displacement, and fears of abandonment in children. She advocates
telling child patients as much as they want to know about the baby.
Such issues as who will be caring for the baby were seen as
particularly important, being thought to express a child's displacement of personal worries or identification with the baby. Nadelson et
al. (1974) discuss the child's accusations that the therapist is not a
good mother. This is difficult for the therapist, who during her
pregnancy is coming to terms with her own maternal identity. In
addition, these authors cite the frank questions children ask about
sex and the physical aggression that may emerge as a result of their
jealousy of the baby.

Fenster (1983) discovered some trends among those therapists
who treated adolescents. The most commonly noted phenomenon
was the high level of adolescent patients' involvement in the pregnancy. This was particularly true of female adolescents. Many therapists were surprised by their young patients' repeated wishes to see
the baby after it was born and their requests to babysit. Personal
questions regarding the therapist's experience of the pregnancy—
morning sickness, the therapist's overall well being and health, and
the like—were typical. One therapist described an adolescent girl
who began each session with "How you doin', mama?" Many therapists noted an overt desire on the part of adolescent girls to be
included in the process of the pregnancy. This evoked a sense of
playfulness and even fascination in the sessions.

Adolescent patients in general were seen as "less thrown than the
adults" by the pregnancy. Unlike the adults, they were not panicked
by the changes in their therapist—at least as expressed consciously.
One therapist in Fenster's study described her adolescent patients as
reacting "in an ordinary way; more like I was a neighbor that's gotten
pregnant."

In responding to the frank questions and curiosity of their adolescent patients, the therapists interviewed in Fenster's study saw
themselves as direct and informative. For example, many were
willing to tell their adolescent patients how they were feeling and,
later on, when requested, to answer questions about the baby. Some
were willing to show pictures of the baby if asked. The therapists
used such words as "open," "disclosing," and "relaxed" to describe
their own reactions to adolescent patients.

While a high degree of therapist disclosure and activity is generally a recommended modification in technique when treating
adolescents (discussed earlier), the level of self-disclosure described

by these therapists goes beyond even these recommendations. Although pregnancy may open up new levels of sensitivity and empathy for the therapist, she must be cognizant of countertransference tendencies at this time. Particularly, there may be a preoccupation with her own experiences and an increased narcissim at this critical juncture in her life. As a result, she may feel unusually inclined to share aspects of her life, lessening the likelihood that a patient's inquiries will be examined for their underlying meanings, associations, fantasies, and so forth. On the other hand, being too analytic—particularly with adolescents—may be counterproductive. For example, a therapist in Fenster's study described the case of a teenage girl who repeatedly asked the pregnant therapist if she could see the baby after it was born. Rather than answering directly, the therapist explored the patient's feelings and fantasies about seeing the baby. In retrospect, the therapist felt that this had been an error. She felt that by not directly answering the patient's request to see the baby, she had left the patient with the hope that she could see the baby after it was born and consequently the girl felt rebuffed when this did not transpire. The therapist said that had she responded plainly that she preferred to keep her private life separate, she and the patient could then have dealt with this rebuff when the alliance between them was still solid, before the interruption in treatment.

The pregnant therapist must now—more than usual—balance her own wishes to be less restrained with a tendency to respond analytically and neutrally. Interactions with adolescents at this time evoke a complex train of reactions. In response to the pregnancy, adolescent girls may become more curious about pregnancy and motherhood, more interested in the person of the therapist. Alternatively, some adolescents totally ignore the event. In turn, possibly because of recommended technical modifications but also because of countertransference feelings, therapists may be less restrained and more revealing than usual. Or they may attempt to cling to their privacy by pushing the adolescent patient away by resorting to "analytic" technique. Overall, the therapist must tread a fine line—being less restrained with her adolescent patients, but not so revealing as to intrude unduly upon the patient's self and associations. If handled with forethought and caution, the pregnancy has the potential to evoke a new level of involvement and sharing within the treatment setting.

Alongside the genuine curiosity shown by many adolescent girls, there are transference implications to consider. The patients' queries about the therapist's health are often unconscious attempts to reassure themselves of the therapist's well-being and continued availability. If the therapist is okay, she can then continue caring for and about her patient. Thus, underlying fears of loss and abandonment are often masked by the adolescent's apparent sense of wonderment. These fears emerge more directly as the therapist's pregnancy progresses and the time draws near for an interruption in the treatment. Eventually, more of the underlying fears erupt. One therapist in the study, for example, described her adolescent female patients as generally "more mad and clingy" as time went on.

When feelings of anger or fears of loss cannot be verbalized, adolescent patients may resort to one of two major defensive constellations: emotional withdrawal or acting out. The patient who withdraws emotionally may come to her sessions, but her interactions with the therapist assiduously avoid talk of the pregnancy. Treatment continues around outside events in the patient's life (and appropriately so), but interpretation of derivatives regarding the adolescent's feelings about the pregnancy are met with resistance and denial. One therapist in Fenster's study said she felt a patient to be "half in and half out" of treatment at this time.

Such an avoidance of the pregnancy despite the therapist's efforts to address it, is not in itself problematic—particularly if the therapist remains aware of the patient's need for and use of this defensive withdrawal. It is important to remember that in general adolescents tend to be uncomfortable considering feelings they might have about their therapists. They prefer to feign disinterest while secretly gathering information. One adolescent figured out which car outside a clinic was her therapist's because of the new baby seat. She apparently looked at the car weekly to ascertain, from the toys and clothes in it, whether the baby was a boy or a girl. Only later did she make a statement about the therapist's baby boy, never having asked the therapist what sex her baby was. Thus, she could maintain her separateness from the therapist by not asking or showing interest, while assimilating information about her at her own pace and in private.

Another example of adolescents' apparent unconcern, but secret fascination, can be seen in the following vignette:

> One adolescent therapy group discussed their therapist's pregnancy only in the waiting room—never within a group session. Finally, in the therapist's sixth month, one of the girls told the therapist that she had a question to ask, with only two minutes left until the end of the session. In this way the obvious interest, previously hidden from the therapist, was presented finally at the end of the session as if it were an incidental piece of information to be gathered. Suspecting what the question would be, the therapist said that there were only two minutes

remaining and that the question might be better asked at the beginning of the next group session. Indeed, the next session brought an initial avoidance of the question, but after the therapist reminded the group that there was something one of the members wanted to ask, many of the adolescent girls in the group burst out with "Are you pregnant?" Following this session, interest in the pregnancy ostensibly waned. The group continued its work with few expressed feelings about the subject. Interpretations focusing on their reactions to the pregnancy were most often met with looks of incredulousness. Issues such as prom dates, problems with parents, and the like remained primary.

In this case, the therapist's pregnancy was met with a continuation of business-as-usual. Perhaps the group setting, particularly that this was a mixed group of adolescents, encouraged reliance on peers and a tendency to ignore the group leader—not unusual in adolescent groups in general.

The other major difficult adolescent reaction to the therapist's pregnancy is acting out. It poses a challenge to the therapist's skills, patience, endurance, steadfastness, sense of security, creativity, and more.

The concept of acting out was first applied by Freud as having to do specifically with conflicts aroused by the transference relationship, which were diffused in action outside the analytic setting. For example, an adolescent girl may become pregnant directly because of her transference need to be just like her pregnant therapist (mother).

Later on, the concept of acting out took on a more general connotation having to do with the patient's character structure. Here, acting out is seen to be an individual's overall tendency to replace emotions and ideas of a painful nature with action. The action serves, as it does in the Freudian notion of acting out, to do away with the potential pain related to those thoughts and feelings. However, the emphasis in the latter definition is on the individual's usual proclivity to respond with action rather than on a specific transference-related action. An example of this characterological type of acting out may be found in an adolescent girl's inclination to react at any sign of tension—be it parental conflict or her therapist's pregnancy—by overeating.

Acting out in relation to the therapist's pregnancy, then, can take the form of either or both types, transferential or characterological. The most commonly reported kinds of acting out during the therapist's pregnancy (Fenster, 1983) ranged from lateness and cancelled and missed sessions to failures to use birth control, promiscuity, pregnancy, and termination of treatment.

For adolescent girls, conflicts and acting out around sexuality may emerge directly in response to the therapist's pregnancy. Unconscious strivings to get pregnant, a real danger in adolescent girls who tend to act out, become more potent at this time and have complex meanings. For one patient, pregnancy may mean being like the therapist—the ultimate form of identification, through merger. Pregnant too, the patient will unconsciously never be separated from the therapist whom she is just like. She and the therapist are one. Another patient's pregnancy, however, may constitute the ultimate rejection of the therapist. Through her pregnancy, the patient may be saying, in effect, "I don't need you anyway. I have my own baby." The patient's baby-to-be is, through projective identification, the patient herself. This baby will receive the love and mothering the patient never received from her own mother and, now, will not be receiving from her therapist.

In an unpublished paper, Ponton (1985) has described the dangers of pregnancy in adolescent girls during the therapist's pregnancy. She found what she considers to be a group-at-risk: adolescent girls with a history of acting out whose mothers also demonstrate acting out, particularly of a sexual nature. In addition, adolescent girls who experienced early maternal loss are also at risk of becoming pregnant. Ponton cautions that those treating such a population pay careful attention to the possibility of pregnancy, and she strongly suggests supervision. On the positive side, her patients were able finally to discuss their mothers' difficulties around men and sexuality—resulting in treatment for their mothers. Spurred by the therapist's pregnancy, experiences and memories of early maternal loss emerged as issues within the treatment for the first time. For the patients in Ponton's sample, pregnancy was a means of getting caring and mothering from those around them, most notably from their pregnant therapists.

Blos (1979) discusses the adolescent's girl's wish for a baby as "an infantile desire to re-establish the child-mother unity (merger)" (p. 253) or as seeking the comforts of infantile contact through cuddling and other bodily touching. Their oral needs are gratified in the guise of genitality and heterosexuality. These needs may be frustrated by the therapist's pregnancy, bringing up early longings for holding, comforting, dependency, and the ministering attentions of the mother.

Acting out that results in the termination of treatment is also a potential problem to anticipate when working with adolescents. Lateness to sessions and cancellations may occur more frequently and often indicate the adolescent's negative, ambivalent, or frightened emotions regarding the therapist's pregnancy. These actions may foreshadow an outright termination. It is therefore essential that such minor changes be addressed head on. The following case illustrates this.

> L was the youngest of four children born to devout Catholic parents. She was 13 when she began treatment. She was smoking pot several times weekly and was failing in school. She came willingly to therapy, seeming to be intrigued by the undivided attention she received and talking freely about her pot use, her contempt for boys, and her rage at her alcoholic father and martyr mother. She freely commented on the therapist's clothing, shoes, age, marital status. By her comments, she sought to make the therapist into an image of herself. She saw the therapist as younger than she really was, unmarried, and looking "cool" when she wore snuggish pants, sweaters, and flat shoes. At this point in treatment, the therapist was functioning within a mirror transference, that is, as an object whose sole function was to enhance, accept, and affirm L's budding self. (See Golombek and Garfinkel, 1983 for a discussion of this aspect of the treatment with early adolescents in general.) L's acting out (pot smoking, school failures, cutting) was a general character style that warded off her feelings of emptiness, confusion, and anger at her parents. L complained constantly of being bored—with friends, boys, school, and so on. After several months in treatment, however, her cutting stopped and she began to voice a desire to be a psychologist and do well in school.
>
> When the therapist became pregnant, about one year into the treatment, L began to miss sessions. When she was confronted about several misses, L said that she was bored with therapy. She wanted to stop coming. Thinking that L might be responding to her pregnancy, the therapist asked if something had changed to make L feel like leaving. L asked if the therapist was pregnant and, after some initial solicitude, launched over the next several sessions into put-downs of the therapist's rounded body and maternity clothes. She particularly focused on the fact that the therapist's hips were no longer skinny. For L, the therapist's pregnancy was a narcissistic disappointment, a break in the therapist's ability to "hold" empathically as before. The differences between the therapist and L could no longer be denied, and the therapist's function as a mirror for the patient had been shattered. L did insist on ending treatment. However, several months later, after the birth of the therapist's baby, L returned.

In this case, the emergence of the therapist as a sexual woman was frightening to this young adolescent girl, who was struggling to hold on to her own androgyny. Fears related to her mother's submission to her alcoholic father, particularly her mother's many pregnancies, emerged, as did her contempt for women. Once the therapist could again be restored as the androgynous self-object (after her pregnancy), the patient was willing to return. It is probable that the therapist's aggressive confrontation of L's missed sessions and wish to leave treatment enabled L to feel recognized and wanted, leading her eventually to resume therapy.

The adolescent girl's idealization of and merger with her therapist, when this is a dominant factor in the treatment, is particularly at risk during a therapist's pregnancy. While the therapist is often viewed as a role model with whom to identify (as in the examples cited earlier in this chapter), it is also possible that an adolescent patient will react vehemently to this disruption in her ability to see the therapist as part of herself, like herself, or there only for her. The resulting breakdown in the adolescent's ability to use the therapist in this way must be handled with the following in mind: 1) the adolescent's rage at the therapist for deserting her, for changing, for introducing the issue of sex; and 2) the adolescent's retaliatory wish likewise to desert the therapist by termination, pregnancy, cancellations, and missed sessions. In addition, wishing to terminate because of anger, the adolescent girl may turn away from the therapist as a result of her narcissistic loss and disappointment. The therapist may no longer be viewed as the same, reflecting, stable object. At the same time, the therapist herself is adapting to changes in her own identity, physiology, and emotions, which ground the adolescent's sense of loss and instability, at least in part, in reality. The therapist may indeed be preoccupied, for example, and this—to even the slightest extent—will be perceived by some patients as boredom, disregard, loss of interest, or, worse, abandonment. The intimate interaction between the therapist's minutest of changes in attention or body, paired with the adolescent girl's need for an object with whom to identify and interact, provides a potentially combustible therapeutic situation.

SUMMARY

We have maintained that both the pregnant therapist and her adolescent patient are embarking upon an adventure of change and a shake-up of identifications. While for most adolescent girls such alterations go on underground, with little disruption in functioning, many situations present themselves that can be either directly or indirectly traced to feelings, fantasies, or conflicts associated with the therapist's pregnancy. Handled forthrightly, with a level of awareness of one's own part in the patient's reactions, the analyst's pregnancy will enhance and deepen the already dramatic sense of sharing and mutuality that working with adolescents, particularly adolescent girls, entails.

CHAPTER 8

The Pregnant Therapist as Group Leader

Five women and four men sit together in a therapy group. They have been meeting for two and a half years. One of the women shares her fears and resentment toward the leader for leaving. She reminds the group that the leader has chosen to leave. Other members of the group work anxiously to deny these feelings, reassuring each other that the leader will return and the group will continue. Two members share formerly unrevealed incidents from childhood in which their parents had become unavailable and depressed over hidden personal loss. The group discusses their discomfort with mourning. It is the final session preceding the group therapist's maternity leave.

As documented and described in this volume, the therapist's pregnancy has a decided impact on the therapy process (Lax, 1969; Paluszny and Poznanski, 1971; Benedek, 1973; Underwood and Underwood, 1976; Clarkson, 1980). The study of transference, countertransference, resistance, and technique issues surrounding the therapist's pregnancy confirms its powerful and complex effect on the analytic space. In these writings, however, the focus has been on individual therapy. Comparatively little consideration has been given to the effect of the therapist's pregnancy on analytic group therapy. This chapter examines and begins to elucidate the impact of the therapist's pregnancy on the group treatment process.

Breen (1977) considers differences between individual and group therapy in connection with the therapist's pregnancy. She reports that whereas individual patients react to the pregnant therapist with concerns about intrusion and sharing in the individual therapy situation, group patients respond in group with family themes and sexual issues. She proposes that the individual and group therapy situations represent two historically different types of past experience. Individual treatment represents an early mother–infant relationship, whereas the group symbolizes a child–family situation. Breen believes these differences account for the variation between individual and group patients in response to the pregnant therapist.

Part of the difficulty in conceptualizing the impact of the therapist's pregnancy on the group may lie in the varying perspectives of group psychotherapy. Some group proponents support a direct translation of psychoanalytic technique to the group situation, calling forth an individual-within-the-group perspective (Freud, 1921; Wolf, 1950; Wolf et. al., 1972). Others consider group dynamics, intervention, and therapeutic change from the group-as-a-whole perspective (Bion, 1952; Durkin, 1964). Alonso and Rutan (1984) offer object relations theory as a way to expand the understanding of group therapy. They consider that in addition to the operation of psychodynamic theory, each group member's response reflects an attempt to modulate separation anxiety while integrating a sense of self and others. Both individual members and the group-as-a-whole use the context of the group to parallel the striving for object relationships and the movement through the schizoid, paranoid, and depressive positions that originally transpire between infant and mother. Group analysts like Ezriel (1950) allow for a combined recognition of the dynamics of both the individual-within-the group and the group-as-a-whole. Ezriel hypothesizes that in individual and group treatment all material reflects the patient's transference and can be understood in terms of three kinds of relationships: the one the patient feels required to have; the one the patient avoids but desires; and the calamitous one the patient anticipates. Ezriel sees the material produced in group therapy in terms of individuals' transferences as well as common tensions and group transferences. Durkin (1981) has applied general systems theory to group psychotherapy such that the whole group, individual members, and their internal representations are viewed as hierarchical subsystems of the larger group system.

Intrinsic to any of these frameworks is a perception of the role and function of the leader within the group. Whether perceived as ego-ideal (Freud, 1921), observer (Bion, 1952), omnipotent mother (Durkin, 1964), transference object (Ezriel, 1950), or identification figure (Kissen, 1976), the pregnant therapist imposes her personal life on the group's perception of herself as leader. The self-revelation implicit in the physical state of pregnancy alternately validates, amplifies, contradicts, or negates the therapist's former personal and professional place in the group. Regardless of the therapist's theoretical orientation, her pregnancy is a significant and complex event that has an undeniable effect on her role as leader. It is an event that reverberates in the feelings and reactions of individual members and the group-as-a-whole.

The impact of the therapist's pregnancy on the group treatment process is discussed here in terms of clinical material drawn from a therapy group conducted by one of the authors. Because the formal orientation was psychoanalytic, the group was conducted with a recognition of the importance of the unconscious, a consideration of transference and historical determinants, the use of free association, and the analysis of resistance. Within this analytic frame, the group leader conceptualized and responded to the group process in terms of intrapsychic dynamics, object relations theory, and group-as-a-whole issues. Her position reflected a belief in the multiple levels of group process and the curative potential for the patient of analyzing and understanding different aspects of self within the microcosm of the group.

The group had been in existence four months at the time of the therapist's pregnancy. There were seven group members (five women and two men), ranging in age from 20 to 45 years. Diagnostically the group was varied. One female member had a history of psychotic depression and, although in remission, she had more difficulty functioning than other group members. Two of the members, a male and a female, were functioning in the neurotic range. The remaining four were considered personality disorders. All group members were in both individual and group treatment with the therapist. All but one member had been in individual therapy for a year or more before beginning concurrent group therapy.

A group's response to a significant, observable group event, such as the leader's pregnancy, parallels, symbolizes, or highlights other dynamics in the history of the group. In this case, the leader's pregnancy was experienced and later discussed as a replay of the feelings evoked in many of the patients when they first entered group therapy, that is, when their individual therapist became, in addition, their group leader. With the pregnancy, they again experienced anger toward a less available therapist (parent); anxiety about sharing, competition, and replacement; and conflicts and fears regarding separation and abandonment.

As a result of the group leader's pregnancy, the common experience of such feelings heightened them and allowed for their eventual ventilation in an atmosphere of mutual validation. It became safer to talk about feeling abandoned, of losing one's special place, of being angry with the leader, when others were openly empathizing with

this response. Working through these feelings, and their unconscious and historical determinants, became an important individual
and group therapeutic experience.

Another effect of the group leader's pregnancy was the disruption
of the existing group process and the crystallization of a more
cohesive and better defined group identity. Whereas the leader's
pregnancy stimulated unconscious conflicts, escalated anxiety,
evoked character defenses, and altered the multiple transferences of
individual group members, the commonality of this impact at the
same time united the group. The group emerged with its own entity,
demonstrating group needs, group transferences, and group resistances beyond those of the individual members. From an object
relations perspective, the group came to serve as a valuable holding
environment, at times replacing the leader as the good mother.

The group leader's ability to recognize and conceptualize the
impact of her pregnancy on the group-as-a-whole, as well as individual group members, is important to the effectiveness of this process.
Regardless of the theoretical frame, recognition of this group phenomenon offers another level of emotional understanding for group,
for individual patient, and for group leader. It underscores the group
as a therapeutic resource with far greater potency than dyadic
relationships. It reaffirms the interpersonal and transferential potential of the group as an arena for reworking personal and familial
dynamics in a different way than in individual treatment. Because
the group leader is often concerned that her pregnancy will result in
the disruption and possible dissolution of the group, recognition of
the group as a powerful entity is important for her and therapeutic
for her patients.

BION'S THEORETICAL FRAMEWORK

The theory of Wilfred Bion (1959) is used here to conceptualize the
impact of the group therapist's pregnancy on the group. Bion's
framework is compatible with psychodynamic and object relations
formulations, while providing probably the best established perspective for the workings of the group-as-a-whole.

Bion defines a group by its task or function. A collection of
individuals becomes a group, and is working, when it demonstrates
consciously motivated behavior directed toward task implementa-
tion. The work of the group is impeded by what is called the "basic
assumption mentality"—undeclared beliefs by members of the
group that the group has met for some purpose other than the

accomplishment of its task. The three basic assumptions that impede a group are: dependency, pairing, and fight-or-flight.

Dependency is operative when the group behaves as if it had met in order to be sustained by an external leader on whom it depends for nurturing and protection. The group members act as if they know nothing and need to depend on an omniscient, omnipotent leader. Pairing is operative when two members in the group pair off, and the group acts as if something magical and curative will emerge from this union. An essential ingredient of the pairing assumption is unrealistic hope and expectation. The fight-or-flight assumption operates when a group behaves as if it had met either to fight or to run away from somebody or something as a way of dealing with stress. Action and panic are the ingredients of this basic assumption.

Bion believes that all individuals have a propensity for combining with the group to become active observers or expressors of the different basic assumptions operative at any given moment. He calls this propensity a valency. A person's valency to respond with one of the basic assumptions is a function of the member's own needs as well as the group's perception of these needs. Group members fit each other and the therapist into unconscious themes and roles. A group's expression of dependency, pairing, or fight-or-flight is the group's resistance to the work at hand. Shifts in these assumptions occur over the course of a group's work and are usually a function of the anxiety and need gratification of group members or the group-as-a-whole. That the adherence to, or shift from, one basic assumption to another is generally outside the group's awareness emphasizes the unconscious aspects of group life.

CLINICAL MATERIAL

At the time of the therapist's pregnancy, the group being considered here seemed to be operating from a dependency assumption. The group, in existence for seven months by the end of the therapist's first trimester, behaved as if it was meeting to be nurtured and protected by the leader. Rarely would they direct questions of importance to each other or feel confident giving an opinion without asking or deferring to the leader. Even as they focused more upon each other, the nature of the group's cohesion was their common need to depend on, and obtain more support from, the leader.

This need for dependence became embodied in one group member. This woman was unconsciously assigned the role of the dependent, "sick" patient. At 28, she was one of the youngest members and the only one who had been hospitalized for mental illness. Her history of psychotic depression, her experience of shock treatment in years prior to this treatment, her overt expressions of depression, anxiety, and occasional looseness of thought and affect both angered and frightened the group. Setting her up as the patient "to be cared for" met her defensive, infantile needs. It relieved the group's anxiety by allowing a means of vicariously satisfying their dependency on the leader. Their focus on the "sick" member and their efforts to have the leader meet her needs were consistent with their emotional assumption but interfered with the real work of the group. It allowed them an avenue for denying the seriousness of their own pathology and resisting engagement in the group process.

The leader's pregnancy disrupted this basic dependency assumption of the group. On a conscious level, the pregnancy threatened the group's child-like sense of self-importance ("How can you do this without asking us?); their expectations of availability and nurturance ("You'll never be able to work like this when you have the baby!"); and their child-like dependence ("What are we supposed to do when you go off to have this baby?"). On an unconscious level, the pregnancy colored the transferences to the leader with associations and images of mothers, babies, siblings, sexual women, and other men's wives.

The group's initial response was denial of the pregnancy. Until almost the sixth month, there was no mention of it in the group. There was collusion in this denial of reality, a tacit agreement to proceed as if the pregnancy did not exist, as if nothing were changing. In a sense, for the dependency assumption to be maintained, the pregnancy had to be denied. As the reality of the pregnancy became more difficult to deny, the group became demanding and angry with the therapist for not properly caring for group members, for not knowing enough, and for not relieving their symptoms. The leader's continuing queries about how these feelings were related to her were overtly ignored.

The actual recognition of the pregnancy and a group discussion about it came as a result of one female patient's announcement that she was so anxious, she could no longer remain in the group. In an individual session prior to this group session, this patient had asked the therapist if she was pregnant. She reacted to the therapist's affirmation with anger, panic, and then guilt about her expressed feelings. When in the next group session this patient announced that she could no longer remain in group, the leader again asked if this had anything to do with feelings about herself (leader). The patient responded with a disclosure of the pregnancy to the group.

According to Bion (1959), this patient's conscious recognition of the pregnancy touched her "area of concern," her preoccupation with finding and possessing an all-available mother as a way of feeling whole and intact. As a result of the pregnancy, the patient feared she could no longer depend on the leader and experienced a sense of abandonment. She could no longer deny the existence of the pregnancy; to remain connected to the group, she needed to make the pregnancy known. Feeling she had lost the therapist, she could not tolerate being in an isolated position within the group.

The leader's affirmation of her pregnancy in the group session had an immediate impact on the group's cohesion. Within that very session, there was evidence of disruption. Interaction by group members moved abruptly from a group to a leader focus. Members stopped talking to one another and addressed all remarks to the leader. Members verbalized their individual reactions to the leader's pregnancy. Perhaps, feeling the panic of losing the group leader, they needed to reaffirm an individual connection with her. For some, this meant regressing to an earlier insistence on being special, with a temporary inability to relate to other group members.

The group's behavior from the time of the affirmation of the pregnancy (sixth month of pregnancy) to the therapist's interruption of treatment for maternity leave reflected a shift from a dependency to a fight-or-flight assumption. This shift occurred because the dependency assumption no longer served the group's needs. Dependency as a means of resisting therapeutic change had stopped being comfortable, had stopped working. Faced with the leader's pregnancy, the group could no longer maintain the dependency assumption embodied in the "sick" member. There could no longer be the fantasy that when they (symbolized by the sick member) were in need, limitless supplies would come from the leader. As a group, they became anxious and increasingly intolerant of the sick member. They responded as if this member were a drain rather a source of vicarious fulfillment.

In group process, when too much anxiety or guilt is aroused in a group by a member being used for the expression of a need, that member is attacked or rejected (Borriello, 1976). In this situation, the group colluded to act in attacking (fight) and then ignoring (flight) the "sick" member. The group members berated her for not grasping what they were saying, for not changing, for being weak. Absorbing their attack, she became confused by the group's comments and interaction and began to speak of herself as "too sick" and "too different" to be in the group. Unable to deal with her own need to be an infant, unable to maintain the position of infant in the group, and unable to compete with the leader's real baby, the patient terminated shortly after the leader's return from her maternity leave. She could not contend with the group's attack and could not find a new, emotionally tenable role for herself in the group. Essentially, the group dealt with their inability to rid themselves of the therapist's baby by sacrificing the group baby. She had become the object of the group's displaced rage at the real infant, the leader's baby.

The leader recognized the group's response as displaced anger toward herself. It was she, not the "sick" member, who hadn't grasped what the group wanted, who had disappointed them, and whom they were unable to change. She had had the audacity to disrupt the group's fantasy. She had become too real to fit their basic assumption of total dependency. Throughout the group's struggle with the scapegoated member, the leader attempted to redirect the group's focus and rage toward herself and away from the scape-goated member. She made the assumption that all content was transferential and listened and commented from that perspective. Gradually, she intervened with straightforward interpretations of the group's anger and disappointment as more likely meant for herself as leader. This permitted an exploration of the feelings underlying the group's displacement. The group was helped to explore their percep-tion of the pregnant leader as different, fragile, and vulnerable, and their fear that confronting the pregnant leader would destroy her. They better understood their efforts to avoid responsibility for the abandonment and loss they felt.

OBJECT RELATIONS FRAMEWORK

A group's reaction to an external event like the group leader's pregnancy, which becomes part of the internal history of a group, reveals important information about the group. The group's confron-tation of, resistance to, and integration of the event, for example, reflects the level of object relations of individual members as well as of the group as a whole.

The authors found that the application of object relations theory to group functioning is effective for a number of reasons. It enlarges the therapist's psychodynamic understanding of individuals in the group process. It provides a frame for conceptualizing impressions and hypotheses regarding the group process before, during, and after the event. And it helps the pregnant group leader re-establish her sense of self as therapist. Often the group leader becomes so em-meshed in the perception of her pregnancy as disruptive to the group that she begins seeing herself as a problem for the group. She loses sight of her role and effectiveness during and beyond the pregnancy. She overlooks her ability to use the reactions to the pregnancy as a valuable reflection of group functioning. Her use of a theoretical frame helps the group leader separate herself from the event and provides a cognitive task that re-establishes her role as therapist and re-aligns her feelings and perceptions of self. Furthermore, the object relations frame of reference, which identifies infant dependency and separation anxiety as primary to the ego's strivings, is particularly relevant because of the infant–mother symbolism of the pregnancy and the reality separation of the group therapist when she has her baby.

CLINICAL MATERIAL

Having experienced the leader's first pregnancy, the group considered was faced two years later with her second pregnancy. The group's response to this event further delineates the impact of a leader's pregnancy on an analytic group, as well as the changes and growth prompted by a group's experience of such an event.

Generally, this group as an entity was functioning at a higher developmental level than it had been two years earlier. It was less leader oriented and seemed to have made beginning strides in resolving early dependency needs and issues related to authority figures. There was evidence of increased trust, a sense of group identity, and movement towards a more advanced developmental phase of intimacy and interdependence (Bennis and Shepard, 1956). The atmosphere and interaction of the group reflected experience and cohesion. New members were more easily assimilated and, on their entrance, explicit and implicit group norms, expectancies, and rules of conduct were communicated. The wish for an exclusive relationship with the leader was more easily given up by members in exchange for the family atmosphere of the group. The leader herself was less active and made more group interventions than she had two years prior.

For the first four months of the leader's second pregnancy, no mention of it was made by group members in either their individual or their group sessions. As the leader's sense of being ignored increased, the group became more cohesive. They were depending on each other for support and need gratification. In the fifth month of the pregnancy, group members were gathered in the waiting room prior to a group session when a member who was returning after a month's absence announced, upon seeing the leader, "She's pregnant again!" The announcement stimulated open discussion, questioning, and affirmation of the pregnancy in the group session. It also came to light that the group had been discussing the pregnancy without the leader present for at least two months in the waiting room!

The group's manner of resisting—withholding of awareness and discussion of the pregnancy from the leader—reflects the group's hidden fears and anger. It also underlines the cohesiveness of the group in resistance. It took an outsider, a returning group member, to verbalize overt awareness of the pregnancy in front of the leader.

The nature of this defense reflects the group's struggle and striving for emotional separation and growth. By becoming a leaderless group in the waiting room, the group took control of their fear of the pregnant leader's imminent separation. They effectively cut off, and unconsciously killed off, the bad, abandoning therapist-mother.

In object relations terms, the group's response represents ego growth. Whereas the group had responded to the affirmation of the leader's first pregnancy with fragmentation and a regressive demand for individual merger with the leader, the group now contained its anxiety by splitting: by ignoring the bad, abandoning leader-mother and working to maintain the group as the all-good, available substitute. To maintain this split, the group refused to validate fears and negative feelings of individual members. There was instead an insistence that the group could take care of everyone and a denial of the reality that the group would not be meeting during the maternity leave.

Under ordinary circumstances, the perception and response to the group as mother is a recognized group phenomenon. Scheidlinger (1974) suggests that on a conscious level the group represents a source of need satisfaction, while unconsciously it may represent an exclusive union with the preoedipal mother. Gibbard and Hartman (1973) consider the perception of the group as a benevolent maternal figure to be a way of defending against the experience and expression of oedipal, libidinal, and aggressive feelings in the group. When the leader is pregnant, this maternal group transference may be further heightened by the reality of the leader as "mother-to-be." A group's need to deal with a pregnant, changing, abandoning mother-leader may prompt the perception of the group as an idealized, all-available, mother.

The power of the leader's pregnancy to evoke responses that then become analyzable and therapeutic is reflected in this group's developmental movement. The group's initial response to the second pregnancy was evocative of paranoid object relating, with splitting off and projection of anything bad as a way of maintaining a good, cohesive sense of self. Over the course of the pregnancy, the group was increasingly able to tolerate and integrate mixed feelings for the pregnant group leader. This ability to tolerate an ambivalent perspective with respect to a parent (group leader) shows the group's movement to a depressive position of object relating (Alanso and Rutan, 1984). There is the experience of self and other as separate and human. With this awareness come the feelings of loss of the idealized parent (group leader) and the idealized group self.

Consistent with the group's increased self-awareness and focus on the less than idealized pregnant group leader was the group's increased sense of sadness and loss in the final trimester. In the last session before the leader's planned leave, the group focused with intensity on some themes of mourning and loss in relation to parents and children. With tears shared by many group members, one member revealed the loss of her family in concentration camps. Another shared for the first time her sense of loss in relation to the death of a ten-year-old sister when she was five. With the help of the leader, the group brought these experiences back to loss within the current situation. The group discussed their fears of the leader's unavailability, her lack of interest, and her possible death in childbirth. As they ended the session, they moved to a consensus about the discomfort and pain of mourning. In so doing, they faced their own resistance to mourning the group situation, for what it once was and what it had come to symbolize.

SUMMARY

The pregnancy of a group therapist, perhaps unlike any other event in a group's history, has tremendous significance. It inevitably alters the therapist's personal, professional, and transferential position in the group. It intrudes on the entity of the group, both in affecting and reflecting the group's process, and alters its developmental level. By its very reality, the group therapist's pregnancy turns up the volume on those issues intrinsic to group therapy—dependency, idealization, merger, separation, abandonment, loss, re-birth, and interdependence. It raises the potential for pain as well as growth as it demands from the group the consensual validation of a shared life event.

CHAPTER 9

Supervising the Pregnant Therapist

It often happens that a therapist is in training, or chooses to be in private supervision, when she becomes pregnant. Probably little in the therapist's learning or experience has prepared her for the often varied, unexpected, and challenging reactions engendered by her pregnancy. There is both rationale and need for seeking the support, feedback, and advice of colleagues and supervisors at this pivotal time in one's own life.

If a therapist is not already in supervision, the choice to enter it during pregnancy is motivated by many factors: first, there is new concern about emotional changes in one's self, one's professional interests, and one's career at this time; second, patients are experiencing myriad and multilayered reactions to one's pregnancy, which may elude or confound the therapist at a time when physical and emotional demands on her are at their peak; and, finally, alterations occur in the treatment process itself, resulting from the therapist's now exposed sexuality, marriage, motherhood, and full life apart from her patients. Indeed, at this time, for these reasons and many others, there is not only a wish but a sense of urgency to consult with others, through either formal or informal channels.

However, this helping process, the very act of consultation during pregnancy, is often fraught with the same complex relational patterns that characterize the process of therapy itself during a therapist's pregnancy. That is, the issue of the pregnancy and the often special needs of the pregnant therapist are evocative stimuli to which supervisors (as people) may find themselves unwittingly reacting. The therapist's new role, the impingement of the pregnancy on the analytic relationship (introduced by the therapist herself), the therapist's vulnerability at this time, the many unknowns—all these can cause the supervisory process, like the treatment process, to take on new dimensions.

A consideration of the impact of the therapist's pregnancy on the supervisory process has been minimal in the literature. Only two articles address this issue directly (Baum and Herring, 1975; Butts and Cavenar, 1979). These authors examine the often negative impact of supervision on the pregnant therapist from the point of view of interpersonal dynamics and its intrapsychic ramifications.

This chapter aims to explore the complexity of the supervisory process as it unfolds and to underscore the immense potential for learning inherent in the conflicts, feelings, and fantasies that emerge in all involved parties during supervision. It is the authors' point of view that, more than being just an arrangement, consultation at this time presents the pregnant therapist and her supervisor with an unusual opportunity. If the supervisory process itself can be used as a tool (on a par with transference, countertransference, dreams, free association and resistance), it may offer up essential—and often preconsciously known—information about a parallel process that may be occurring between patient and therapist. Indeed, during the therapist's pregnancy, supervision encompasses a unique set of relationships among therapist, supervisor, patient, and baby. The difficulties observed in the supervisory process at this time may originate in this four-way arrangement. To view the process, as other writers have (Baum and Herring, 1975; Butts and Cavenar, 1979), as existing only between supervisor and pregnant therapist overlooks the potential richness of the supervisory experience.

Baum and Herring (1975) cite a tendency on the part of neophyte therapists to deny that their pregnancy posed difficulties for their patients and themselves. They point to the therapists' wishes for understanding and their attitude of "business as usual." These tendencies are seen as the result of intrapsychic conflicts within the pregnant therapist, leading to such emotional reactions as guilt and anxiety. Baum and Herring also suggest that the supervisor's anxiety, hostility, and jealousy may interfere with the supervisory process during the therapist's pregnancy. Male supervisors in particular may not be aware of the physiological aspects (such as fatigue, nausea, bouts of hunger and weakness, muscle strain, edema, difficulties sleeping) and the emotional factors (such as changes in identity, guilt feelings, need for support) that may effect the pregnant therapist.

Butts and Cavenar (1979) discuss how therapists' anxiety and denial about their pregnancy in treatment can lead to their missing patients' references to the pregnancy. However, those authors assert that such conflicts arise as a result of peer and supervisor reactions. They present a series of clinical vignettes that drive home their point that supervisors and peers may unwittingly create intrapsychic conflict for the pregnant therapist. Examples of supervisory sadism, lack of empathy, condescension, and patronizing attitudes are given.

PARALLEL PROCESSES

Fifteen of the 22 pregnant therapists interviewed in Fenster's study (1983) were in supervision at the time of these (first) pregnancies. In examining the results of the interviews, Fenster found that the therapists had unwittingly described some striking similarities between their interactions with patients and with supervisors. Indeed, many of the feelings and the impasses experienced with patients during the pregnancy seemed also to be occurring in supervision. In most cases, these parallels were not explicitly described by the therapists but rather were implicit in the material. It is remarkable that in no case were these parallels between the therapeutic and the supervisory processes actually discussed within supervision.

Before we describe these parallels in further detail, a look at the literature on parallel processes is warranted. Many authors have reported and discussed such similarities between the supervisory and psychotherapy situations in other contexts.

Searles (1955) saw it as a "reflection process." The therapist makes an unconscious identification with the patient and in supervision attempts to communicate the nature of the therapeutic problem to the supervisor. The therapist unconsciously identifies with a part of the patient or with a conflict that the patient cannot put into words. The therapist then communicates what has been experienced with the patient by "acting it out" with the supervisor. In Searles' thinking, the process works predominantly in one direction—the therapist brings the patient's problems into supervision and plays them out.

Ekstein and Wallerstein (1958) view the same process as an interaction between therapist and supervisor. They describe a meshing of transference and resistance patterns between therapist and supervisor that may parallel problems between patient and therapist. They see a parallel between therapists' difficulties in therapy and their learning problems in supervision. The supervisor is viewed as an active participant in an affectively charged helping process. Insight into the interplay of forces between the therapist and the supervisor is seen as essential for learning to take place.

These writers see the supervisory process—its problems and interactions—as providing important, perhaps unconscious, information about the therapeutic process. As such, the supervisory process itself offers another dimension for analysis and understanding.

Doehrman (1976) studies in more detail the interrelationship between supervision and psychotherapy. In a series of interviews and rating forms, she examines the interactions between two supervisors, four therapists, and eight patients. Her findings suggest that tension in the supervisory relationship is inevitable. If this tension is understood and managed skillfully, it can be an important facet of the therapist's professional growth. This involves the supervisor's addressing himself or herself to the therapist's emotional reactions to both the patient and the supervisor. For treatment to remain unjeopardized, Doerhman found that supervision had to be more than just a didactic or consultative experience. In addition to affirming Searles' hypothesis that therapists temporarily identify with their patients and play out the patients' impulse-defense patterns, her research also confirms the idea that the parallel process works in the other direction as well. That is, supervisors stir in therapists reactions they then "act out" with their patients. Doehrman's research points to the reciprocal nature of the supervisory parallel process—experienced by both therapist and supervisor and inevitably affecting or reflecting the treatment of the patient.

Along the same lines, Lesser (1983) suggests that "if anxieties inherent in the supervisory situation are not appreciated, they may interfere with the goals of supervision" (p. 121). Lesser recommends a "collaborative-coparticipant model" (after Wolstein, 1981) where there is inquiry into both the supervisor's and the therapist's transference and countertransference, which can be directly experienced and observed within supervision. She quotes Gediman and Wolkenfeld (1980), who emphasize that parallel processes do not originate solely with the patient, but are the product of "multiple identificatory processes" within the supervisor–therapist–patient network. For example, Lesser writes that the supervisor may dissociate anxiety-provoking aspects of the relationship with the therapist.

PREGNANT THERAPISTS AND THEIR SUPERVISORS

In the vignettes that follow, the "multiple identificatory processes" described by Gediman and Wolkenfeld (1980) may be observed in action within supervision. However, when the therapist is pregnant, the triadic relationship described by them (supervisor–therapist–patient) is not sufficient for understanding the multifaceted reactions taking place. Indeed, supervision of the pregnant therapist involves a fourfold system—that of the therapist, her supervisor, her patient(s), and the feelings and fantasies of everyone about her baby.

Discomfort

Many of the therapists interviewed (Fenster, 1983) described a sense of feeling less open, more distant, and newly uncomfortable with their supervisors since their pregnancies. In discussion, it emerged that these therapists perceived their supervisors as having difficulty with their pregnancies, particularly within the realm of the supervisor's possible envy or jealousy.

Three therapists, for example, had single, female supervisors with whom they felt distinctly uncomfortable during their pregnancies. Would the supervisor's envy or jealousy, actual or fantasied, interfere with or spoil their collaborative process? One therapist voiced it this way, "I couldn't believe that we were still going to be able to work together" (Fenster, 1983, p. 113). The same therapist, at another point in the interview, had described concern about a single, female patient whom she was seeing. This patient had always been competitive with the therapist, and now her envy of the therapist's pregnancy was emerging. The therapist feared that the patient might use the interruption in treatment, when the baby was born, "as an excuse" to terminate. The therapist, likewise, was concerned that she and her supervisor might not "be able to work together." These were parallel concerns—that the supervisor and patient, particularly with regard to their envy, would not weather the issues that arose with the therapist's pregnancy. The therapist, however, was unable to voice her feelings in supervision—particularly regarding her uncomfortableness with both her single, female patient and her single, female supervisor—thereby placing both treatment and supervision at risk. Compounding the therapist's discomfort was the supervisor's inability to perceive and address what became both a transference and a supervisory issue: envy.

Another therapist in Fenster's study, whose supervisor had "talked about wanting a baby . . . before I was pregnant and during" (Fenster, 1983, p. 113), felt discomfort in bringing up patients' issues with the supervisor which specifically had to do with her pregnancy. The supervisor "indirectly made it clear that these are not topics she wished to pursue in depth . . . I felt her uncomfortableness which

made me want to back away from it" (Fenster, 1983, p. 113). This
therapist, in the course of the interview, also discussed her own
tendency to "back away from dealing with [her pregnancy with
patients] because I was uncomfortable to bring too personal issues
into the treatment" (Fenster, 1983, p. 113). She felt, in particular,
that she was having difficulty handling her female patients' envy and
jealousy. She said she could have done more to "reach out" to one
female patient, to discuss what the patient was feeling about the
pregnancy. She described yet another patient as having simply
"backed off, she just didn't talk" (Fenster, 1983, p. 113). This, it will
be recalled, is what the therapist herself had said she had done with
her female supervisor: she had protectively backed off from engaging
the supervisor in issues surrounding the pregnancy, so as to avoid
confrontation with the supervisor's real or imagined envy. Indeed,
had the supervisor been more aware of her own feelings and felt able
to discuss them with the therapist in supervision, important learning might have taken place. The therapist might then have been able
to transfer this willingness to confront envy to the treatment situation with her patient. More specifically, she might have learned that
envy and jealousy need not be tip-toed around but could be discussed, tolerated, and contained within the ongoing relationship.

Another therapist in the study was planning to take an extended
leave from her clinic position and her patients there. A majority of
therapists in the study took such maternity leaves, either planned
before the delivery or unexpectedly extended afterward. This therapist described her relationship with her female supervisor as "protective" because she "had a lot of feelings about my leaving and it
made me very hesitant to be as open and direct as I wanted to be
with her" (Fenster, 1983, p. 114). The therapist felt that she would
have benefitted from more intensive supervision during her pregnancy and leave-taking. Here, the parallel difficulties surrounding
the issue of leave-taking in both supervision and therapy went
unexplored. The therapist's protectiveness toward her supervisor
precluded her getting the help that she needed regarding her patients. Moreover, these very feelings about leaving might have been
more explicitly addressed and handled by her supervisor—possibly
leading to the therapist's increased ability to handle this event with
her patients at a very crucial time.

As is evident from the three cases just cited, these therapists were
reflecting, in their discomfort and withdrawal from their supervisors, similar interactions occurring with their patients at that time.
Had they been able to discuss their feelings, or had their supervisors
been more willing to probe for their own and the therapists' feelings,

these supervisees might have experienced a greater sense of mastery over the very difficult issues of envy, jealousy, and leave-taking to which their patients (and they) were reacting. It is also noteworthy that the therapists and supervisors often resorted to defenses similar to those used by the patients—avoidance, denial, oversolicitousness, suppression, repression, and reaction formation. Supervisors in the examples did not address the therapists' resistances to these issues in treatment. Nor did they broach their own feelings or thoughts, proving resistant themselves, within supervision. Although it is the supervisor's role to point out vulnerabilities and omissions, emotionally this was not possible in the cited cases because of similar vulnerabilities and omissions on the part of the supervisor. The supervisor's "crisis" set off a similar "crisis" in the therapist, and vice versa.

Sensitivity to Criticism

Another issue that cropped up in both supervision and the analytic relationship was the therapist's increased sensitivity to criticism. Baum and Herring (1975) have cited the pregnant therapist's increased need for support and understanding, needs and feelings that were also reported by the therapists in Fenster's study (1983). This has particular ramifications within the supervisory dyad. The pregnant therapist's sensitivity to disapproval or criticism in supervision may also parallel a vulnerability in the patient–therapist dyad. Therapists reported reacting more strongly to increased anger or blame from patients as well as to disapproval from supervisors. Their strong reaction made it more difficult to explore these emotions objectively and intensively within supervision. Possible underlying feelings of resentment or irritation on the part of patients thus may be glossed over by the therapist. As a result, patients may go underground with their anger, saving it up for the time when the therapist returns from her maternity leave, or terminating treatment abruptly as a result of it. Or the anger may be turned into solicitousness or protectiveness through a process of reaction formation. These styles of reacting to the pregnancy may be accepted uncritically and remain unexplored by a therapist who is feeling her own unsettled emotions at a time of vulnerability and change in her own life. (It must not, however, go unsaid here that such reactions of solicitousness on the part of patients may be genuine acts of concern and caring. This will be addressed later in the chapter).

The therapist's need for nurturance and support must be understood by the supervisor. The supervisor should be open to exploring points at which the therapist may have been too sensitive or reactive, or where she is perhaps colluding with a patient in avoiding his or her anger. But, more important, anger, blame, or criticism may also occur within the supervisor–therapist dyad. The supervisor may become more critical at a time when changes are occurring rapidly in the treatment situation. The therapist may indeed be somewhat preoccupied. Or the supervisor may become more protective of the therapist in an effort to save her from an awareness of her shortcomings or to shield her from reality in some countertransferential blunder. Why might a supervisor unwittingly become more critical or protective at this time? The situation may be one with which the supervisor may have had no prior experience or which may create a feeling of inadequacy. The supervisor may experience anxiety, or even panic in the face of potential expectations or the reality of the therapist's new dependency needs. The supervisor's reaction is a function of his or her own dynamics regarding the therapist's pregnancy or pregnancy itself.

In the foregoing examples from Fenster's work, the supervisory process became constricted and inhibited during the therapist's pregnancy. Rather than enriching the therapeutic process, supervision hindered it. There was, on all sides, a distancing, a withholding, and a fearfulness that were never addressed and understood in their larger context—that of the therapy relationship with the patient.

Given these issues, the supervisor's willingness to discuss these tendencies and feelings in supervision can be invaluable in understanding the similar feelings of criticism, anger, and blame of patients toward the pregnant therapist.

New Closeness

Apart from these stresses, positive interpersonal processes in supervision occur regularly at this time. These may also offer important information about the therapist's relationships with her patients. For example, several therapists in Fenster's study (1983) discussed their feelings of a new sense of closeness with their supervisors. The supervisors were experienced as more giving or real within the supervisory relationship during the pregnancy. They shared more freely in advice-giving and in personal anecdotes about their own children, adding a new dimension to the supervisory relationship. This process mirrors the experience of some therapists in the study who felt that they themselves had become more real, more human with their patients during their pregnancies. They found that they answered more questions, were more verbally active, and were less likely to refuse gifts than they had been in the past.

An example of this new give and take can be seen in the following case. The therapist, who was pregnant, was seeing a male patient in analysis who alluded many times during her pregnancy to the inability of his mother to accept gifts from him. The mother would accept nothing other than "abject dependence" from him. One day, when the therapist had difficulty opening a closet door that had gotten stuck, the patient opened it for her. In the several sessions that ensued, the patient associated repeatedly to this interaction, feeling a sense of warmth and great caring for the therapist, who had allowed him to give her this "gift." Later, in describing her supervisory relationship, the therapist noted similarities between this occurrence in the therapy and a similar one in the following supervisory hour. The supervisor went overtime and suggested an article for the therapist to read, both unusual actions for this often "strictly analytic" supervisor.

Attachment and Dependency

Another common positive interaction occurring in supervision during the therapist's pregnancy is the therapist's new feelings of attachment and dependency on the supervisor. Therapists found (Fenster, 1983) that their reliance on a supervisor increased over time as more and more was occurring within the treatment situation as a result of the pregnancy. They looked to supervisors more directly for advice, help in understanding, and feedback. This process reflects a similar one occurring with patients. Many therapists described a new awareness of attachment and dependency on the part of their patients since their recognition of the pregnancy. Such positive feelings had theretofore been unexpressed or avoided within the treatment by many of these same patients. Thus, the pregnancy—and perhaps the fantasy that the therapist might be "leaving" in some sense because she was having a baby—enabled patients to get in touch with their own, previously unrecognized, deep attachment. An awareness that such a process might be occurring in supervision, and a discussion of its meanings and ramifications, would have aided in elaborating and uncovering such processes of attachment within the therapeutic dyad.

Clearly, there is a therapeutic advantage to the new sense of attachment, responsiveness, and closeness that may emerge within the supervisory and therapeutic relationships during a therapist's pregnancy. Its presence reflects quite vividly similar emotions of caring, warmth, and involvement within therapeutic and supervisory interactions.

Reparative Moments

Moreover, such feelings of closeness represent reparative moments of concern. These reparative moments were deeply recognized and felt by the therapists in Fenster's study. They were moments that often sustained the therapeutic relationship and allowed further mutual exploration of sadistic, envious, or angry feelings. Similarly, in supervision, this kind of exchange can eliminate the fear of nonacceptance. The supervisor's role expands to respond to and accept the therapist. A very primary emotional need is being met within supervision. This can enable the therapist, who is physiologically and emotionally in transition, to deal more effectively with her patients.

Other Dynamics

In addition to the foregoing, there are of course other kinds of dynamics between therapist and supervisor that may parallel those with patients. Some of these are sexual feelings of attraction or disgust, devaluation or idealization of the therapist, and maternal transference to the therapist. These dynamics can be experienced by both supervisors and patients—providing the supervisory dyad with an opportunity to explore and understand often nonverbalizable feelings and fantasies.

FEMALE AND MALE SUPERVISORS

Another issue that emerges as important at the time of a therapist's pregnancy is whether there may be differences in the help one can get from a female versus a male supervisor. This question was implicitly and explicitly raised by many of the therapists in Fenster's study. As always, the answer is complicated and individual to each person's needs. However, some trends may be pointed out that also bear on the parallel process paradigm being considered in this chapter.

Some therapists (Fenster, 1983) who had had male supervisors during their pregnancies voiced, in retrospect, a wish for a female supervisor, especially one who had been through the experience of pregnancy herself. In particular, whether or not the supervisor was a *parent* seemed crucial in the choice of supervisor—male or female. Thus, even where there is a stated desire for a female supervisor, it may be more salient to consider whether the supervisor or the supervisor's spouse has gone through the experience of pregnancy and birth.

A study by Ingber (1981), however, suggests that there are notable differences with male and female supervisors. Ingber found that female psychiatric residents (not pregnant) tended to use their supervision with female supervisors quite differently than they did with male supervisors. The important distinction was the extent to which female supervisors and supervisees were willing to discuss mutual role and personal issues within supervision. This did not occur as often with male-paired supervisor–supervisees in her study. Ingber felt that female residents wanted a female supervisor in order to have someone to "model themselves after, emulate, and identify with in integrating their professional and personal identities" (Ingber, personal communication, 1983).

In line with Ingber's findings, it is of interest that many pregnant therapists voiced a wish for a female supervisor (Fenster, 1983). Also, a large majority of therapists turned to female peers who have had children for help with cases independent of whether they are also in supervision. Because of the crucial role modifications that occur with the coming of one's child—especially when one intends to continue in one's professional role—the need to turn to another woman who has successfully negotiated similar experiences may feel urgent. Being in supervision with such a person, in particular, seems to offer not only the prospect of good training and guidance but the chance to consolidate professional role and identity issues as well.

In a kind of parallel process, many female patients look to their female therapists as role models. Therapists in Fenster's study often noted that their pregnancies seemed to provide many of their childless female patients with a chance to experience a woman as both professional and mother.

One therapist described a patient who had rejected the feminine role and saw marriage as a trap. The patient "was very curious all along about the pregnancy . . . seeing me go through it at close range was relieving. . . . The pregnancy allowed the patient to feel more feminine. She felt that [pregnancy] might be an okay thing to do. I went back to work. I didn't die. I could laugh about it. I liked the result" (Fenster, 1983, p. 72). As described earlier, some female patients, often those unmarried and without children, began (as a result of their therapist's pregnancy) to grapple more directly with fears and ambivalences regarding childbirth, children, attachments to men, and career.

In sum, just as female therapists use their female supervisors as role models (Ingber, 1981), so female patients may also look to their female therapists as role models. And this may be particularly true when the therapist is pregnant. The wish to identify with and be transformed by the model provided by a significant object seems to be quite strong at this time for both therapist (in supervision) and patient (in therapy).

GUIDELINES FOR SUPERVISION

When the therapist learns that she is pregnant, or sometime soon thereafter, the supervisor and therapist should spend a block of time simply talking about the pregnancy. To focus on the pregnancy in such a direct way is to recognize and acknowledge the central importance of this event in the therapist's life. Following this, a careful consideration of each patient's dynamics in light of the issue of the pregnancy is warranted. These discussions should take place, if at all possible, before the pregnancy becomes known to the patients. Discussions should include a review of the patients' major areas of conflict, their usual defensive styles, how the patients generally deal with separation, displacement, anger, and abandonment, and expectations for how patients might go about handling the fact of the pregnancy. For example, might a patient become withdrawn, oversolicitous, jealous; might he or she resort to acting out such as pregnancy, hypersexuality, and the like?

Because many of the therapists in Fenster's (1983) study felt that transference issues, and the real relationship between patient and therapist, had become more focused and central to the work during the pregnancy, it is also recommended that these issues be addressed systematically and on a regular basis over the course of supervision. Here it is particularly relevant that supervisors be aware of their own feelings and reactions to the therapist, her pregnancy, and her baby. They must observe how these may be enacted in the supervisory sessions and utilize these data as a potential point of reference for understanding the therapists' or the patients' dynamics.

Areas of potential parallel phenomena were outlined earlier in

this chapter; they include envy, jealousy, feelings about the therapist's leave, anger, disapproval, protectiveness, wishes to share
experiences, feelings of attachment, caring, distance, idealization,
maternal transference. Shifts in the "feeling" of supervision, the
level of tension, or comfort, for example, might also be thought about
in terms of what may be occurring in therapeutic relationships at
this time. Both positive and negative reactions and interactions hold
useful and often untouched information within them. Supervisors'
exploration of their own feelings will insure a facilitation of the
supervisory process rather than an acting out or mutual denial of
underlying issues.

Within this context, supervision can have tremendous impact on
the pregnant therapist. It can provide her with a unique cognitive
and emotional support system. It can be a growth experience for all
involved. It is an opportunity to learn and to give. An examination of
how the multifaceted issues discussed here affect the four-way
relationship of patient–therapist–baby–supervisor, in all directions
and manifestations, seems not only warranted but necessary.

CHAPTER 10

The Homosexual Patient and the Analyst's Pregnancy

For the homosexual patient, the analyst's pregnancy is a particularly complex event. Theoretical and clinical material reveals that few other situations in the life of the analyst touch so closely upon the homosexual patient's own unconscious conflicts and issues. This chapter examines the reactions of the homosexual patient to the pregnant analyst in terms of patient dynamics and treatment issues.

Homosexuality is defined here as a sexual orientation in which the preferred mode of achieving sexual satisfaction is with a partner of one's own sex. According to the *Diagnostic and Statistical Manual of Mental Disorders*, (DSM III) (American Psychiatric Association, 1982), homosexuality is not automatically considered a manifestation of mental disorder. It is diagnosed as an indication of mental disorder when it causes a person significant subjective distress.

For purposes of this study, the term homosexual includes people who define themselves in terms of a sexual preference for partners of their own sex and who are suffering significant distress in relation to their sexual preference or acts. These are persons for whom homosexuality is ego-dystonic or disagreeable to their sense of self and identity. Also included here are people who define themselves as homosexual but who present themselves for treatment because of an intolerable but undefined anxiety or a crisis in some other aspect of their lives. Their wish is often to maintain their sexual preference while ridding themselves of the attendant anxiety.

THEORETICAL CONCEPTS

Freud's (1905) "Three Essays on the Theory of Sexuality," initiates
the theoretical treatment of this subject. Freud assumes that homosexuality is an acquired characteristic of the sexual instinct deter-
mined in early childhood. By 1910, he considers identification and
repression as playing an important part in homosexuality. Freud
holds, for example, that the male homosexual never relinquishes the
early attachment to mother and continues the attachment by identifying himself with the female. Eventually, Freud (1919) comes to
consider homosexuality as a defense against castration anxiety. For
the male, the wish to replace father and love mother is felt to escalate
the fear of castration by father, so that the boy develops a negative
oedipal reaction. He regresses to an earlier identification with
mother as a way of retaining her without reprisal from father.

For the female, Freud (1933) considers that the feelings of inadequacy and castration that prompt the girl to want father, to have his
penis, to have his baby conflict with her wish to depend on and be
gratified by mother. If at puberty the girl's own libido is so overly
repressed by fear of retaliation by mother and by disappointment in
father, she will be unable to establish a sexual identification with
mother. She will instead identify with father, avoid heterosexual
desires and maintain a safe, childlike position with mother.

Other theorists, such as Deutsch (1932) hold that the female
homosexual choice is an attempt to alleviate guilt arising out of rage
at mother. The girl blames mother for her castrated female self and
for mother's masturbatory prohibitions. At the same time, the girl's
homosexual choice protects her from disappointment in father, who
never came to her rescue.

For Fenichel (1934), the female homosexual is unable to go on to
another man because of fear of retaliation by father. Instead, she
chooses a female love object as a representative of herself, loving the
representation in the way father should have loved her. Also, according to Fenichel, the female homosexual's choice and pattern reflect
the oral eroticism of infancy, the mutual playing of mother and
child.

Socarides (1978) proposes that there are different forms of clinically overt homosexuality. Pertinent here is his differentiation between oedipal and preoedipal homosexuality. In oedipal homosexuality, the oedipal complex and castration fears lead to the adoption
of a negative oedipal position; that is, the male assumes the role of
female with father (other men), and the female assumes the role of
male with mother (other women). Gender identity has become

disturbed because there is a secondary identification with the person (parent) of the opposite sex instead of the same sex. Homosexuality is an attempt to insure dependency while acquiring power by seducing the more powerful same-sex parent. Preoedipal homosexuality implies a pregenital fixation on mother, which generates tremendous anxiety regarding loss of self and ego bounds. Here homosexuality becomes a means of stabilizing a sense of self. For the preoedipal male, the weak masculine sense of self needs sexual connection with a male partner to insure masculinity and avoid engulfment by mother. For the preoedipal female, an unacceptable female self, derived from fixation on a hated mother, necessitates sexual connection with another female partner to re-create a good and reparative mother–child bond.

In conceptualizing the dynamics of homosexuality, there has been considerable focus on the role of aggression. Nunberg (1938), who holds that homosexuality stems from aggressive and libidinal drives, proposes that homosexuality reflects restraint of aggression or the disguised expression of it. Melanie Klein (1954) considers the earliest aggressive impulses, and their defensive introjection and projection, as basic to the development of homosexuality. Rosenfeld (1949) asserts that homosexuality may serve as a defense against paranoid anxiety arising from intense aggression. In his work, Bychowski (1956) refers to homosexuality as a regressive adaptation that originates in excessive early stimulation of aggression and turns hate into love. Stoller (1975) suggests that homosexuality may involve a fantasy of childhood revenge, motivated by hostility.

TREATMENT ISSUES

The interaction of the homosexual patient's dynamics with the event of the analyst's pregnancy is reflected in the principle elements of the analytic treatment process: the working alliance, transference, and resistance.

The Working Alliance

In order that analysis proceed, a patient must be able to engage in a nonneurotic, rational working alliance with the analyst. The desire to relieve anguish and pain prompts the patient to cooperate with the process and procedures of treatment. Many patients, criticized and misunderstood by the outside world, come to treatment with fears and assumptions of rejection. For homosexual patients this is often consolidated in the belief that the "straight" analyst will be unable to empathize with their homosexual choice or their distress about this choice. There is often the fear that the "straight" analyst will threaten the only type of relating or sexual pleasure they have known.

The pregnancy of the analyst is undeniable proof of the analyst's heterosexuality. The contrast of this reality with the homosexual's own sexual choice, in the context of the analyst's pregnancy, often precipitates a disruption in the working alliance. There is a re-emergence of fears and assumptions about the "straight" analyst. Even where a strong working alliance exists there may be acting out, devaluation of the analyst, apathy, and threats to terminate. In cases where treatment has recently begun, there is often insufficient trust and experience within the alliance to contain the homosexual patient's feelings and reactions to the pregnancy. Still other patients, despite the length of time in treatment, are unable to maintain a rational, asexual, unaggressive alliance in face of the sexual and aggressive stimuli of the analyst's pregnancy.

Transference

Transference, in the broadest sense, signifies the extent to which the patient's experience of the analyst is colored by feelings, impulses, and defenses originally directed toward others, generally the significant persons of early childhood. Theoretically, the anonymous, nonintrusive status of the analyst, teamed with the judicious use of transference interpretations, exposes the distortion and projection inherent in the patient's transferential perceptions, which are henceforth relinquished. In reality, the here-and-now relationship between the patient and analyst often lends some plausibility to the transference. Accordingly, transference is here considered to be a function of the patient's intrapsychic determinants in conjunction with the purposeful or inadvertent influences of the analyst (cf. Gill, 1984).

The pregnancy of the analyst has a major impact on the transference. For both male and female homosexuals, the analyst's pregnancy evokes a range of feelings and projections. The now-pregnant analyst may become an object of love, hate, sexual attraction, castration fear, or identification.

Although this influence on the transference is significant for all patients, it is particularly disruptive for the homosexual patient whose pathology is a function of early developmental defect. These homosexual patients often develop narcissistic transferences in which they demand merging and mirroring. Ordinarily, the analyst allows this type of transference to develop, acting as the container and mirror for projections. The pregnancy of the analyst, however, overtly interferes with this mirroring function.

The analyst's now obvious sexual difference is perceived by some homosexual patients as withholding, abandonment, even annihilation. Patients may respond to this breakdown in the mirroring function with anxiety and rage. This rage is at times exacerbated by the conscious or unconscious fantasy of the analyst's merger with her baby, rather than with the patient.

In responding, the analyst, with empathic listening, accepts and contains the patient's rage and attendant anxiety. Where appropriate, she validates the patient's feelings and perceptions, and then with analytic inquiry invites the patient to consider what else might account for his or her experience of the analyst at this time. Such questions as "How will my pregnancy make me unable to respond to you?" "How does my sexual preference change me here?" "Must sexual difference imply desertion or dismissal?" become valuable to the analytic process.

By supporting the patient's ego in the examination of projections and reactions, the analyst allows the patient a nonjudgmental arena for rage and anxiety while experiencing the analyst's continued presence and emotional involvement.

For the female homosexual, the analyst's pregnancy often initially heightens a positive transference. The female homosexual, often pursuing the idealized mother-child relationship in her lesbian attachments, becomes excited and preoccupied with the pregnancy as an emotional solution. In terms of her projected identification with the analyst, the pregnancy invites the female homosexual into the mother–child bond. In the transference, it allows her to be the idealized mother to the vulnerable pregnant analyst, or to be the child to the idealized mother analyst. In oedipal terms, the analyst's pregnancy allows the patient symbolically to have father by having his child or to replace father by having this child with the analyst/mother. The female homosexual's unconscious solutions thus allow her for a time to feel relief from anxiety while remaining dependent on the pregnant analyst/mother.

This heightened positive transference gives way to fears of losing mother and being replaced by baby or father. In the transference, there is eventually an anticipation of rejection and exclusion by the analyst/mother. This is consistent with Eisenbud's (1982) position that the experience of maternal exclusion is basic to the female's lesbian choice. By taking a female partner, the lesbian uses the erotic bond with another female to replace the early maternal absence. The analyst's pregnancy in this context may come to represent the original exclusion and rejection by mother. Escalating rage and fears of abandonment, the maternal figure of the present becomes too much like the maternal figure of the past.

A major aspect of the male homosexual's response to the pregnant analyst is the fluctuation between preoedipal and oedipal transference feelings. The homosexual male patient unconsciously wishes for but fears merger with mother. The pregnant analyst therefore becomes a complex and anxiety provoking transference figure for him. She can be an all-giving mother who at the same time threatens engulfment, as well as a sexual mother who provokes the wish to replace father while implying, in her pregnancy, her connection with a more powerful, potent man. Such transference projections escalate tremendous anxiety. Whereas the female homosexual patient has more emotional leeway for adapting to or identifying with the pregnant analyst, the male homosexual faces emotional annihilation—loss of self or castration anxiety on either the preoedipal or the oedipal level. He is left with rage and despair, which generates guilt and further anxiety as he struggles to defend against the negative transference. If the negative feelings become unmanageable for him, he will be unable to rely on his own defensive style and the result will be an emergence of formerly disguised, more regressive personality patterns.

An example of a male homosexual patient's transference response is examined in the following case:

> Shortly before a male homosexual patient became consciously aware of the analyst's pregnancy, he began having sexual dreams involving men he didn't know and with females all around him—students, neighbors, colleagues. Such dream material seemed reflective of his efforts to repress heterosexual drives and fears heightened by the unrecognized pregnancy. Concurrent with his open recognition of the pregnancy was the repeated presence in the dreams of the analyst's husband, whom the patient had never seen. The reported dream image of the patient as an intruder who mistakenly enters the analyst's home instead of the office and who fears discovery by the husband, whom he observes with the analyst at a distance, is strikingly oedipal and evocative of castration anxiety.
>
> Paralleling this on a conscious level was the patient's personal contempt for and denigration of the physical appearance of the analyst during pregnancy. This underscored his attempt to resolve the oedipal trauma with devaluation and withdrawal from mother. In the patient's

words: "I am unable to feel any connection to you. I feel no sexual attraction. I feel repulsion to pregnant women." Eventually, the patient's anxiety became so disruptive that there was an increase in the amount of primary process material in the sessions. He vacillated between rage at the therapist and fear of her retaliation. He reported shame for his hidden wish to poison the analyst and her baby, while at the same time fearing that she was "pregnant, dirty and could contaminate" him.

For some patients, like the man discussed above, the pregnancy of the analyst induces a regression that is potentially disruptive to the analysis. In such cases, alterations in analytic technique become necessary to respond to the patient and preserve and facilitate the treatment process. For the patient just described, a decrease in the number of sessions, accompanied by systematic undoing of his projections, acknowledgment of the reality aspects of his perception, and active reassurance that he would not "poison" the analyst reduced the regression and helped reestablish a working alliance.

Resistance

The homosexual patient's anxiety aroused by the analyst's pregnancy and the complexity of positive and negative feelings stirred warrant the analyst's alertness to resistance.

For both male and female homosexual, for example, positive feelings toward an overtly heterosexual analyst may be very anxiety producing. Such feelings trigger castration anxiety, expectations of parental retaliation, and even fears of engulfment and loss of self. Positive feelings of identification and attachment to the pregnant analyst are, thus, often resisted with apathy, withholding, verbalized contempt for analyst and treatment, sexual promiscuity, lateness and missed sessions, and threatened termination.

Negative feelings toward the pregnant analyst also provoke conscious and unconscious resistance. Rage toward mother being central to the unconscious dynamics of the male and female homosexual, it is inevitable that it will erupt in response to the pregnancy of the analyst. The homosexual patient resists awareness of these negative feelings to avoid retaliation and abandonment by an angry mother and to prevent anticipated destruction of mother and consequently of self. Defense against negative feelings often includes denial, projection, reaction formation, acting out, distance, or avoidance of treatment. If too much anxiety is created, the patient may show such signs of regression as intolerable anxiety, paranoid ideation, bizzare acting out, somatic complaints, aggressive outbursts, and, ultimately, dissolution of treatment.

The pregnant analyst must counter this resistance to effectively move the treatment forward. With disruptive regression, the initial goal must be the reduction of anxiety and use of the patient's ego for self-observation and analysis. For acting out, it may be necessary to use reality confrontations, directive interventions, and parameters within the treatment to prevent self-destructive or treatment destructive behavior.

Where acting out is unlikely, the pregnant analyst confronts the resistance with empathic listening, clarifications, and analytic inquiry. As in any analytic work, it is important to recognize that premature or excessive confrontation may engender more rage and escalate anxiety if it generates guilt, shame, and self-recrimination. The impending separation from the pregnant analyst, who will soon interrupt the treatment to have her baby, may not afford the time and pace to allow the resistance to emerge as obvious and dystonic to the patient. In some cases, the impending separation may create a crisis atmosphere such that characterological resistance is confounded by situational panic and therefore is beyond the patient's self-awareness. In these cases, the pregnant analyst may use empathic, clarifying interventions to reduce anxiety, while postponing a fuller analysis of the resistance for the return to treatment after her maternity leave. It has been observed that after treatment resumes following the maternity leave, there is often initial relief and reconnection by the patient, followed by a reemergence of the resistance.

CLINICAL CASE

An illustration of the impact of the analyst's pregnancy on the homosexual patient is provided in the case of R.

R entered treatment at age 26 because of considerable anxiety and depression she could no longer mask with drugs and alcohol. She could not relax and felt "out of control" and despairing.

R defined herself as homosexual, having a sexual preference for and involvement with women that began during her college years. Central to R's anxiety and despair at the onset of treatment was a relationship with a new lover whom she described as overtly feminine, well educated, brighter than she, and from a wealthy family. R vacillated between feelings of grandiosity and inadequacy in the relationship. At times, she boasted about her lover's good looks and overt loyalty despite male attentions; at other times, she anxiously awaited abandonment by this woman. R was sensitive to her lover's moodiness and very threatened by her lover's male analyst.

R's anxiety was further heightened by her feelings of rage and attraction toward a male employer who both exploited her and depended on her. She was easily seduced into overwork for this man's praise but was often disappointed and enraged when he fell short of her idealized expectations.

The analyst became pregnant seven months after R's twice-a-week treatment began. Part of R's entry into treatment reflected a wish to compete with her lover's male analyst by merging with an analyst of her own. Her choice of a female analyst was an emotional necessity, as she feared being the weak, dependent female in a relationship with a male. In the relationship with her female analyst, R expressed the wish to be nurtured, the fear of rejection, and the need to be "pseudotough" and controlling.

In the first weeks of treatment, R reported this dream: "I was chopping up my parents, putting them in a shoe box and stuffing it on top of a closet." The dream reflects the magnitude of R's rage and her strong need to "stuff" it away. As reenacted early in the transference, emotional survival necessitated placating and seducing the female (mother), while avoiding the male (father).

The determinants for R's rage were a childhood of neglect and physical abuse at the hands of a controlling, angry father and a weak depressed mother. R was the middle child, with a brother one year older and a sister ten years younger. Although both she and her brother suffered the consequences of their father's violent temper, she perceived her brother as being mother's favorite and sought to emulate and please him. This led to sexual exploitation by him in her early teen years.

When R was ten, her mother became pregnant with her younger sister. At the time of her sister's birth, R's life changed drastically. Her father left, her mother became depressed and suicidal, and R was sent to boarding school. Her brother, whom she described as more manageable, remained with her mother and the infant sister. From that time, R proceeded through school and college with some financial support but almost no relationship with family members.

R was aware of the analyst's pregnancy early in the first trimester. Vigilant to any nuance of change in the analyst's response or manner, R dreamed that she was "in a new situation in which something happened that I couldn't fix." Soon after this, R openly asked the analyst if she was pregnant. She responded to the confirmation with excitement, personalized overinvolvement, and anxiety. With a sense of euphoria, R spoke often of the expected baby and insisted it would be a boy.

Identifying with the analyst, R experienced the pregnancy as unconscious fulfillment of the wish to have the male baby (penis) she longed for. At the same time, the pregnancy became a shared event in which she was the fantasied male counterpart to the female analyst as symbolized in talk of "their baby." These dynamics were central to the euphoria she experienced.

On a more conscious level, the pregnancy heightened R's anxiety, as her wish to identify and connect with the pregnant analyst evoked her historical attachment to a pregnant mother. In R's emotional frame of reference, pregnancy meant depression, threats of suicide, and abandonment by a mother figure. The wish to identify thus became extremely anxiety provoking. This conflict was reflected in R's increased coolness within the treatment and her preoccupation with the pregnancy outside of treatment, where, she reported, she thought incessantly about the pregnancy and involved her friends in frequent discussions about it.

In the second trimester, R's preoccupation with the pregnancy subsided. She refocused on issues of her personal life and seemed to be less anxious. Responding to the positive, nurturing aspects of the transference, she appeared less emotionally needy. Her previous efforts to monopolize the treatment session with soliloquies or instructions to the analyst were reduced, and her demand to be the constant center of attention with lover and friends abated.

In the last trimester, transference issues again took over. R reported the following dream to the analyst:

> You call me and I'm at my sister's house. I ask how come you called and cancelled. You say you are transferring me to someone else . . ., Then I'm speaking with my dead grandfather. I try to call you back but I can't find your card so I look you up under the address of a Dr. Jones. . . . I'm with a man at a Holiday Inn. I tell him I have to find my doctor. . . . There are glass doors. I see you laying on a couch away from the window. You have a broken leg. You are only wearing a towel. I am sitting on a step near you. You tell me I have to go. You are rushing me out because your husband is coming. He comes in and passes by me. You kiss him. I say "por favor."

The dream reflects R's terror at the analyst's upcoming separation to have the baby. Her association is of death and damage in the image of her dead paternal grandfather, a loving, attentive figure who disappeared after her father left, at the time of her mother's pregnancy. R's inability to reach the analyst in the dream, "I can't find your card," echoes her expectation of the finality of separation. The heterosexual strivings symbolized by the dream image (being with a man at a Holiday Inn) defend against her despair and panic at being unable to remain attached to mother. Historically, and as expressed in the dream material, the heterosexual choice is an untenable one for R. She moves from involvement with the man to an identification with a castrated, helpless mother/analyst. The erotic connecting, the wish to be included sexually with a woman, becomes a way of withstanding being cast out by mother. R anticipates no response to her wish to be included by mother. In the dream, there is no response to her words, "por favor"—"please."

In the last month of the analyst's pregnancy, R was notably withdrawn and depressed. She described herself as "frozen and frightened." Both historically and in the transference, R's depression defended against the powerful rage she felt, this time at the analyst. Her fear of annihilation as a result of the analyst's imminent separation and her belief that her rage could destroy the analyst were reflected in a dream reported three days before the analyst gave birth:

> I am down south with my father and his new wife. There is another house there with a man, woman and a child. They go into town and their house burns from the bottom up. There is only the skeleton of a house left. I think they are inside and I get twigs to build a step so they can get out. I wake up in a sweat.

Working with this dream, the analyst actively supported R's expression of anger and fear in response to her pregnancy and upcoming maternity leave. She helped R make connections with childhood memories of her parents, their destruction of her childhood, the "skeleton" of a family life she had had, and her rage toward them. In exploring the reality of the imminent disruption (destruction) of the treatment, the analyst reminded R that she planned to return to work with her.

R put herself "on hold" during the two months of the analyst's maternity leave. Although able to function in most situations, she greatly missed her connection with the analyst, crying and withdrawing somewhat from friends. She reported thinking often of the analyst and the baby.

It was not until the analyst's return to treatment and R's reassurance of the analyst's well being that she could begin to allow negative feelings to emerge. She needed the repair of a mother who would return in order to begin her own separation. Initially her expressions of rage and disappointment were paralleled by repeated dreams of a woman with five children who becomes her lover. The interpretation and discussion of R's fear of losing the analyst (mother), and her unconscious need to replace her with another mother figure, was valuable in moving the treatment.

Over the course of the next six months, R made significant strides in a growing sense of self. With the freedom to express the early rage, she was no longer depressed and significantly less anxious. Ego growth was reflected in her manner of relating: there was less projection, exhibitionism, and fear of being judged. She changed jobs and seemed less dependent on approval and validation from others. She remained in the relationship with her female lover but increasingly spoke of them as two "women" who were important to each other. There was less merging or playing out of roles. By the time the treatment stopped a year after the birth of the analyst's child, R had begun her own business and was relocating. She spoke with a sense of intimacy and entitlement of having really come to know the analyst, of having "lived through" her pregnancy. In her words, they had both really changed.

SUMMARY

The pregnancy of the analyst is a complex and compelling event for the homosexual patient. First, it is a confrontation with heterosexuality, which underscores the homosexual patient's dystonic experience of his or her homosexual self. Adding to the feared perception of being different from the rest of the world, the analyst's pregnancy confirms her different sexual orientation. Second, the ongoing event of the pregnancy evokes unconscious material, memories, and associations central to the homosexual patient's fears and conflicts. Themes of sexuality, pregnancy, parent–child attachment, separation and replacement, in effect, highlight the patient's unresolved castration fears, early maternal fixations, defensive identifications, dependency needs, and expectations of exclusion. Third, the analyst's pregnancy confronts the homosexual with formerly repressed feelings of rage and loss, now paralleled by the rage and loss felt toward the pregnant analyst.

The impact of the analyst's pregnancy is observable in the elements of the treatment process. The working alliance is inevitably strained by a reemergence of fears and assumptions about the "straight analyst" being judgmental and rejecting. The transference is altered. For the female homosexual, there is often an initial heightening of positive feelings, with the analyst's pregnancy serving the patient's unconscious wish to be included in the perfect mother-child bond or to resolve the oedipal dilemma by symbolically having father's baby through identification with the analyst-mother. This idealized transference inevitably gives way to fears, ambivalence, and negative feelings. For the male homosexual, there is often an immediate expression of negative feelings as the analyst's pregnancy provokes wished for but threatening transference projections. For the male, fears of engulfment and castration escalate anxiety and alter the transference. For both male and female homosexual patients there is a heightening of resistance to the analyst's pregnancy. This is frequently evidenced in denial, projection, sexual acting out, distancing, and avoidance of treatment. Depending on the patient, there may be a redoubling of character defense or signs of severe regression.

The intensity and complexity of the homosexual patient's response to the pregnant analyst need not be an impediment to growth. Rather, the pregnant analyst's understanding and analysis of this response has unique therapeutic potential. The homosexual patient, confronted with the heterosexuality of the pregnant analyst, is at the same time the recipient of the analyst's continued empathy and acceptance. This reality can foster a reconsideration of anticipated rejection, projected rage, and fear of sexual differences, and promote acceptance of self. Similarly, the early childhood memories and associations stimulated by the analyst's pregnancy prompt the reexperiencing and resolution of childhood pain and conflict with a clarity that might not otherwise have been possible. Finally, the time-limited realities of the analyst's pregnancy and maternity leave re-create in reality issues of connection and separation central to the homosexual patient's conflict.

Generally the pregnancy of the analyst is an event that stirs a broad range of past and present feelings in the homosexual patient. The opportunity to ventilate and analyze these feelings with the analyst without reprisal can provide the homosexual patient with a unique curative experience.

Chapter 11

The Impact of Motherhood on the Therapist

Every woman changes dramatically after giving birth. Motherhood involves a reorganization of a woman's self-concept in many areas: her relationship to her own mother, to her husband, to her child and to society. In our culture there has generally been what Leifer (1980) refers to as a "motherhood mystique." This mystique implies that mothers should devote themselves exclusively to the care of their infants, that it is only the mother who can meet, and should meet, the needs of her children. It is apparent that the therapist returning to her practice after the birth of her child is flying in the face of long-held tradition. In addition, she intensifies the conflict that began with her pregnancy—that between being a "good" mother and being a "good" professional. This conflict is unresolvable, and the feeling of perpetual conflict provides a backdrop for understanding the therapist mother. Ultimately, it is perhaps only the acceptance that there will always be conflict between career and child rearing that lessens the emotional strain.

Although trends in society have changed so that many more mothers have professions and work outside the home, society provides little support for the working family. A woman is on her own in arranging child care and organizing all the needs of career, children, marriage, and home. Any one of these can be a full-time job, yet most therapist mothers are faced with all.

Several writers (Benedek, 1959; Leifer, 1980; Rossi, 1968) believe that parenthood is a developmental stage, with the radical changes and opportunities for new integration in personality that this implies. Benedek is particularly eloquent in her description of the

116

emotional symbiosis between mother and child and how this relationship defines the mother's ability to feel that she is a "good" or "bad" mother. The complexity of the interactions, the revival of earliest conflicts in the mother, and the intensity of the emotional relationship between mother and infant are all operating within the therapist as she returns to see her patients after the birth of her child.

The peak emotional stress for the therapist is most likely to occur in the first several months postpartum. It was during this period that most of the therapists in Fenster's study (1983) described themselves as fatigued, preoccupied with the baby to a greater extent than when pregnant, and drained by the baby's demands. Perhaps one of the issues exacerbating the conflict for the therapist is that by returning to work only six to eight weeks after the birth, she is still feeling what Winnicott (1956) refers to as "primary maternal preoccupation." Winnicott describes the prospective mother's gradual turn inward and then her state of heightened sensitivity, which enables her to "adapt delicately and sensitively to the infant's needs at the very beginning . . . to the exclusion of other interests" (p. 302). Winnicott likens this state of sensitivity to a "withdrawn state or a dissociated state or a fugue, or even . . . a schizoid episode in which some aspect of personality takes over temporarily" (p. 302). It is no wonder, then, that returning therapists are reluctant to resume their work, feel apathy for things unrelated to the baby, and wish to remain with the baby. Many therapists in Fenster's study were surprised by the degree of attachment they felt. As one therapist said, "Having a baby is very different from thinking about a baby . . . It's so hard to tear myself away from my baby and concentrate on my patients" (Fenster, 1982).

For some therapists, the intensity of preoccupation is heightened through breastfeeding. Nursing induces an unmatched emotional and physical closeness between mother and child. It is a very sensual and sometimes even a sexual experience. Often, breastfeeding provides the working mother with a haven, an exclusive bond with her baby that helps bridge the time spent apart. At the same time, it can be tiring, draining, and infringe upon one's sense of self. It is worth considering the impact of this absorption on the therapist, who must be attentive in a similar way to the needs of her patients. One therapist (Fenster, 1982) described her predicament:

> In a metaphorical sense, to the extent that there's any feeding that does go on in therapy, it's like breastfeeding and the great demand that it places on you. I think that alot of my exhaustion and fatigue would have been much less had I not been breastfeeding. There's a certain

demand placed on you that you're the only one that can do it. And I think there's some of that on the therapist too."

In the early years of child rearing, the quality of being on call, on demand, characterizes the life of the mother. Feeling on demand is also an underlying theme in the life of the therapist. Containment of an infant's dysphoria, aggression, and disorganization may go on alongside the containment of similar feeling states in patients. There are times when the therapist as a new mother feels that she is doing the same job everywhere. Two therapists, for example, described it this way: "I couldn't tolerate anyone [patients] needing anything from me and they needed alot" and "The worst was that I felt I had very little energy to handle rage from patients" (Fenster, 1982).

The return to work, while inducing stress, also is a stabilizing factor for the woman's self-esteem, identity, and participation in the life of society during a time when her sense of self is shifting in all arenas. As one therapist put it: 'Work provides me with stimulation, a sense of organization, involvement with life and a time frame. With the baby there is often a sense of timelessness" (Fenster, 1982). Although some therapists fall comfortably into the more secluded lifestyle involved in caring for an infant, for others the shift is wrenching, particularly when much of one's sense of identity and self-esteem has come from the achievement of professional activity. For them, working while childrearing can provide essential bolstering and relieve fears about losing professional expertise and confidence.

STAGES IN THE RETURN TO WORK

The therapist as a new mother is experiencing a peak of openness to emotion—her own and her baby's. She is exquisitely sensitive to the baby's needs, moods, happiness, and pain and is necessarily more empathic since much is communicated between mother and child through empathy. Her primary focus is her infant and the powerful feelings engendered by new motherhood. There is an intense need to protect the symbiotic orbit from all impingements. Eventually, every mother must look beyond this orbit with her child. The therapist mother, however, not only must move beyond this orbit but also must integrate her mothering with her professional role. Often she does not have the luxury of moving into her professional role when she and her baby are ready.

Anticipated Loss

The attempt to integrate the roles of mother and therapist can be conceptualized in two stages. The first stage, which we term *Antici-pated Loss*, is characterized by a fear of loss in both spheres of career and motherhood. The second stage, termed *Dual Role Integration*, is characterized by the ongoing struggle to balance both roles comfortably.

In the first stage, Anticipated Loss, the idea of returning to work with patients brings with it dread, anger, anxiety, relief and excitement. There is fear that one has traded in one's ability to be a therapist because of absorption with the baby. There is concern that patients will no longer see one as a therapist. For example, one therapist voiced surprise when all her patients showed up for their initial session after her maternity leave.

Other therapists anticipate coming up against patients' anger that may have been held in abeyance during the last months of the pregnancy and the leave. The therapist may react to patients' questions upon returning as intrusive forays into her cherished and private symbiotic orbit with the baby. In contrast, others may welcome patients' queries, wanting to share their joy and involvement. During this phase also there is a concern that patients will react to one's physical appearance. For example, patients may remark on the therapist's weight, clothing, and fatigue. It is often a wish to look the same and be the same that leads therapists both to want and to dread this kind of exchange.

These first anxieties are part of the stage of anticipated loss. This fear of loss necessarily results from having chosen to be both therapist and parent, and necessarily part time at each. As part-time mother, the therapist fears losing connectedness with her baby, fears the baby's preference for other mothering figures, feels a sense of loss at missing out on the baby's special moments, and fears that her choice will inevitably damage her child's emotional growth and development. As part-time therapist, she fears a loss of connection and effectiveness with her patients, anticipates a loss of patients' commitment to treatment, and fears that her lack of total commitment now as part-time therapist will irrevocably damage her patients. In addition, the therapist mourns the loss of her own immersion in her profession—all the committees, readings, jobs, training opportunities that she had formerly had or anticipated.

Despite the intensity of these fears, it is the actual return and beginning work with patients that allows the therapist to relax and start integrating her dual roles. With even the first patient, there is often a sense of relief and validation of one's continuing ability to be a therapist. No matter how long a therapist chooses to delay her return—seven days, seven weeks, seven months—it is only her return to work that leads her to move beyond the anxieties of this stage.

Dual Role Integration

In the second stage, Dual Role Integration, the therapist repeatedly grapples with the quandary of separation from her baby and reconnection with her patients. To do this, she must be able to move in and out of merger with her infant into a working alliance with her patients. This demands the emotional flexibility to be totally involved, at different times, on demand, and in different ways. She must combat the fear that to be absorbed with one will contaminate her connection with the other.

In our experience, and for a majority of the therapists interviewed (Fenster, 1983), having a baby brought immediate changes in the emotional involvement with work. This was described by some as an initial feeling of "removal," "distance," or "detachment." This initial feeling of removal from patients and desire to be with the baby often developed into a more therapeutic, less merged position vis-à-vis patients. "I used to be too connected to my patients, as if they were surrogate children. Now I seem better able to put the therapeutic relationship into perspective" (Fenster, 1983, p. 100).

This sense of having treated patients as surrogate children, indeed, indulged surrogate children, was often encountered. Once the real child is on the scene, there is less overinvolvement and overinvestment in the therapy child. This shift seems to bring about greater limit-setting and less flexibility regarding appointment schedules, availability for phone calls, payment deadlines, and toleration of abusive behavior. Therapists now have less of a stake in keeping patients when such limits cannot be adhered to.

With the attainment of greater emotional distance, the therapist is better able to stand back and gain a clearer overall understanding of the issues of the patient and of the issues between therapist and patient. The therapist is less enmeshed and therefore is more herself. This, paradoxically, leads some therapists to feel much sharper in their work, more sensitive to patients, and more open. This seems almost in contradiction to, but is because of, the increased sense of distance.

One wonders if the establishment of and increased comfort with boundaries has implications for the therapist as mother. Does involvement with her practice reduce the likelihood of the therapist's becoming overindulgent, overinvolved, and overinvested in her child, enabling the child's increased independence and self-expression? It is possible that, in both directions, the need for a narcissistic attachment is reduced.

As she builds up a continuing sense of her own capacity to shift roles successfully, the therapist–mother finds that she is comfortable bringing her increased emotional openness into the treatment process. She is better able to maintain an empathic stance, to tolerate chaos and frustration without feeling excessively frustrated herself. She can fine-tune her concentration level, and she can use her experiences as a mother as a frame for understanding her patients' needs. Emotionally, she develops the capacity to enter the moment alternately with her baby and with her patient with confidence, ease and trust. She comes to see that her dual role choice can be enriching for herself, her child, and her patients.

As well as extending her emotional capacity, the therapist's parenthood also broadens her experiential frame. She is in a much better position to empathize with a patient's pull toward symbiosis with a child or a patient's feelings of violence toward a child. The number, and at times overwhelming intensity, of emotions engendered by parenthood now become even more comprehensible.

Winnicot (1963) makes the point that in handling the dependency needs of our patients and in protecting a fragile ego from being overwhelmed "there is nothing we do that is unrelated to child care or infant care. In this part of our work we can in fact learn what to do from being parents . . ." (p. 251-252). This observation raises the question of how the quality of the therapist's work changes when she becomes a mother.

Almost all the therapists interviewed by Fenster (1983) reported changes in their empathic responses to mothers, families, and children. There was increased respect for the complexity of feelings and issues between parent and child and between parents. The addition of a child to one's life produces innumerable changes and provides an incredible richness of experience.

The therapist-mother, dealing with her child's dependency, vulnerability, responsiveness, curiosity, and aggressiveness, gains direct access to appreciating the child's needs and living with a person-in-the-making. It is the authors' experience that their having children has made the memories and fantasies of childhood incidents reported by patients much more vivid and vibrant because of a more intense involvement with these experiences. One can wonder whether this enhancement is a permanent addition to the therapist's understanding of human experience or if the passage of time or repression mute the availability of such strong emotional responses. It does seem that the developmental stage of one's own child will have some impact on one's work as a therapist. At each new stage for the child, the mother may go through a revival of her own conflicts during the same stage. This may lead to emotional upheaval; to sensitivity to phase-specific issues, probably reflected in therapeutic work; to the potential for a better integration of the issues; or, to a negative outcome with increased conflict and pathological manifestations.

Other changes that occur as a result of the motherhood of therapists include a new sense of flexibility vis-à-vis patients' knowing personal things about them: "I'm less afraid of patients knowing things about me and my life. As long as it's explored . . . the pregnancy is a public event and once you've experienced nine months with a public event in the room I think it helps you deal with public events. . . . I'm not so crazy and worried about preserving my privacy" (Fenster, 1983, p. 100). For many therapists interviewed, there was an increased sense that patient's knowledge about them could be an impetus for exploring crucial dynamic issues. This is in contrast to the view previously held by many therapists that patients' knowledge about them may have been a contaminant to the treatment. It seems as if the experience of using the issues generated by the pregnancy to enhance the treatment also provided a frame for many therapists within which they felt more comfortable bringing their humanity and active selves into the therapy.

Some therapists experience an immediate shift in their self-esteem and femininity as a result of the experience of pregnancy and motherhood. Therapists in the Fenster (1983) study spoke of feeling more content, more peaceful, and more complete, perhaps as a result of fulfilling part of the role of a woman—creating a child. Certainly birth and motherhood are peak creative experiences that often result in heightened self-esteem.

Before they have children, many therapists invest much creative energy and nurturing in patients and career activities. After the birth of one's own child, some of the need for achievement and creative expression in the outside world may be changed because of absorption in and fulfillment from the child. For some women, this means they table, with minimal conflict, certain professional goals and activities. They embrace the opportunity to be full time mothers with the luxury of time to be with their child. For others, the birth and mothering experience generates a sense of deprivation, resentment or depression about interrupting career priorities.

The fact remains nevertheless that a woman's experience of juggling career and motherhood will always be rife with conflict. The therapist's response to this conflict is likely to be a function of her own personality and her level of achievement. For example, how much a woman has achieved prior to having her child is related to her feelings about interrupting her career. If she feels she has achieved a good measure of success, she may be satisfied enough to feel comfortable about cutting back. If she is just building her career, she may then experience the baby as an interference and the source of intense conflict.

PATIENTS' RESPONSES

How does the patient respond to the therapist's return to work? There are a variety of reactions over time. Initially, most patients seem happy to see the therapist and to varying degrees speak quite directly of missing therapy and the therapist. The behavior in relation to asking about the baby is very mixed. Some patients ask about the baby in the polite way that one might expect—they ask about health, weight, name, and sex, if they do not already know. With many patients, there is no continued questioning about the baby—on the surface, the issue seems to be "dropped like a hot potato." Some patients ask nothing about the baby. One therapist (Fenster, 1983) described a patient who never asked anything upon her return to treatment. On the bottom of her first month's check, the patient's husband wrote the following message to the therapist, "Congratulations on the birth of your son." In fact, the therapist had had a girl. This patient, an extremely narcissistic woman who had twin sons and, according to her therapist, "functions in terms of seeing everyone as a mirror," (p. 96) had simply assumed that the therapist had had a boy.

Perhaps ignoring the issue of the baby is an attempt by patients to reestablish the analytic relationship as a dyad, trying to banish the three-person relationship that came to exist during the pregnancy. Ignoring the issue of the baby upon returning to treatment also is a denial of the existence of the baby rival, who now is not so vividly apparent in the consulting room. This new baby is a very real threat to the patient's feeling of specialness. Although a patient may feel rivalrous with other patients, the therapist's baby is a real insult to the fantasy of any patient's special position.

This denial of the baby's existence is perhaps akin to, or a re-creation of, the young child's wish to kill off, or magically make disappear, the newly arrived sibling. For the patient to focus on the new "sibling" is to be in touch with the intense envy and hatred that might have made the home situation, and now the therapy situation, feel intolerable. Fenster (1983) found that many of the therapists she interviewed were relieved to comply with the patient's avoidance and denial in their own attempts to rectify the integrity of the treatment to return to a dyad with primary focus on the patient.

The attempt at restoring the prepregnancy harmony is partially but never fully successful. As patients begin to perceive the therapist as healed and healthy again, they begin to express a great deal of anger both directly and indirectly. Patients feel "some sense that things are not going to be the same again—something was lost and could never be had again." (Fenster, 1983, p. 98). This feeling of irrevocable loss is important to explore in terms of a transference revival of a sibling's birth or a parent's absences.

There are, of course, many real factors that affect the therapist's availability. After delivery, most therapists make some changes in their office setting, (from home office to outside office or vice versa) their schedules, and their availability for telephone contact. In addition, the "primary maternal preoccupation" of the therapist with her child in the early stages of motherhood may easily be sensed by patients. So while patients are by no means abandoned, their position is realistically and qualitatively different; many sense this (especially borderlines) and react with anger. Patient's jealousy of, and competitiveness with, the baby is often expressed. Themes of wanting to be in the baby's place, or pushing the therapist to choose between baby and patient are common.

> One of the authors had been treating a very disturbed borderline woman, 23 years old, for two and a half years prior to her pregnancy. The patient was transferred to a colleague while the therapist was on a seven-month leave. Upon returning, the patient reported that she was involved with a "wonderful" man who, unlike the therapist, could give her things she really needed in her real life. She described the boyfriend as controlling, potentially explosive, domineering, jealous, and possessive. She alternately reveled in feeling central to him and feared his consuming jealousy. The patient terminated treatment with the claim that she now had a "real life" person to replace therapy and the therapist, just as she felt replaced by the baby.
>
> About two years later, the clinic through which the therapist had been seeing the patient received a confusing letter from the patient. In the letter the patient insisted that the therapist was her childhood babysitter and accused the therapist of denying this. Apparently this

patient had undergone a psychotic decompensation, exacerbated by the therapist's pregnancy and baby. While she was obviously still very attached to the therapist, the envy and rage at being displaced from this "babysitter's" center of attention was emotionally unbearable.

Acting out such feelings at the time of the therapist's return has many of the same qualities as that encountered during the pregnancy: lateness, missed sessions, premature terminations, pregnancies, suicidal threats and late payments.

A patient's reactions to the therapist's pregnancy and motherhood, whether experienced as feelings of displacement by the baby, wishes to replace the baby, or curiosity about the therapist as mother, probably continue as long as the patient remains in treatment. The following case illustrates this issue.

Some two years after returning to work, one of the authors was with a patient who had experienced the course of her pregnancy. This 41-year-old woman had two daughters, each with serious problems. The therapist and patient were discussing one of her daughters, apparently not to the satisfaction of the patient, who shouted "You wouldn't have forgotten how badly my daughter needs help if you weren't so preoccupied with your own child!" Thus the ongoing reality of the therapist as mother becomes the context for expressing dissatisfaction with the analyst, even two years after the return to work.

The public event of the therapist's pregnancy and motherhood, then, inevitably affects the nature of the relationship between patient and therapist. For some, there is a heightened stimulation of maternal transference, issues of rivalry with the therapist's child and competitiveness with the therapist as a mother. For other patients, there is a feeling of mutuality and anticipation of greater understanding for their own position as parents. For yet others, there may be an augmented fantasy of a new beginning with this "good mother." Many other possibilities exist, but certainly nothing is ever quite the same.

ORGANIZING LIFE IS A PREOCCUPATION

The organization of her life is probably the theme of the woman of the 1980s and is certainly the theme of the therapist mother. Scheduling and organizing now must become major preoccupations if the therapist mother is to make her life function smoothly. Primary in this process of organization is the formulation of and comfort with a child care plan (live in, live out, full time, part time, etc.). This usually entails the search for quality child care, a search that engenders as much stress as any major life trauma. It can, and often does, induce stress and regression in the therapist, now dependent on a caretaking person who will replace her in caring for her child. Without a child caretaker, the therapist cannot be a therapist. If the quality of the caretaker is not high enough, if the person is not experienced as an adequate extension of herself, the therapist is caught in a web of guilt, anger, resentment, and self-striving that is emotionally exhausting and damaging to all involved. Since in our society there are no guidelines or cultural support for child care, the therapist mother is on new ground. Like all working mothers, she will come to know terror when the babysitter or housekeeper says she is leaving, is ill, or is dissatisfied, a trauma that generally happens many times during the years when child care is essential.

With all the stresses, adjustments, and upheavals that occur as a result of the decision to have a child, there are changes that one can never anticipate. The authors concur with Winnicott (1963) that so much that we do in therapy is like parenting and that we can learn how to be with our patients from our experiences as parents. Becoming a mother and raising children brings to a therapist an empathy, a sensitivity, an openness, a richness of emotional experience, and practical wisdom that can only increase her effectiveness with her patients. It is difficult to imagine any other life situation that can produce such a plethora of change and learning.

REFERENCES

Alonso A., & Rutan J. S. (1984, November), The impact of object relations theory on psychodynamic group therapy. *American Journal of Psychiatry*, 141:11, pp. 1376–1380.

American Psychiatric Association (1980), *Diagnostic and Statistical Manual of Mental Disorders, Third Edition*. Washington, DC: American Psychiatric Association.

Ballou, J. (1978), *The Psychology of Pregnancy*. Lexington, MA: Lexington Books.

Balsam, R. (1975), The pregnant therapist. In: *On Becoming a Psychotherapist*, ed. R. Balsam. Boston, MA: Little, Brown.

Barbanel, L. (1980), The therapist's pregnancy. In: *Psychological Aspects of Pregnancy, Birthing, and Bonding*, ed. B. L. Blum. New York: Human Sciences Press.

Baum, E., & Herring, C. (1975), The pregnant psychotherapist in training. *American Journal of Psychiatry, 132*, 419–423.

Bellak, I., & Faithorn, P. (1981), Intercurrent events: Marriage, pregnancy, childbirth, divorce, moving, threatening or actual illness, death. *Crises and Special Problems in Psychoanalysis and Psychotherapy*. New York: Brunner/Mazel.

Bender, E. (1975), *The Pregnant Therapist—Outpatient Setting*. Unpublished manuscript.

Benedek, E. (1973), The fourth world of the pregnant therapist. *Journal of the American Medical Women's Association, 28*, 365–368.

Benedek, T. (1956), Towards the biology of the depressive constellation. *Journal of the American Psychoanalytic Association, 4*, 389–427.

———. (1959), Parenthood as a developmental phase. *Journal of the American Psychoanalytic Association, 7*, 389–417.

Bennes, W., & Shephard, H. (1956), A theory of group development. *Human Relations, 9*, 415–437.

Berman, E. (1975), Acting out as a response to the psychiatrist's pregnancy. *Journal of the American Medical Women's Association, 30*, 456–458.

Bibring, G., Dwyer, T., Huntington, D., & Valenstein, A. (1961), A study of the psychological processes in pregnancy and of the earliest mother-child relationship. *The Psychoanalytic Study of the Child, 16*, 9–72. New York: International Universities Press.

Bion, W. R. (1952), Group dynamics: A review. *International Journal of Psychoanalysis, 33,* 235–247.

———. (1959), *Experiences in Groups.* New York: Basic Books.

Bleger, J. (1967), Psychoanalysis of the psychoanalytic frame. *International Journal of Psycho-Analysis, 48,* 511–519.

Blos, P. (1962), *On Adolescence.* New York: Macmillan.

———. (1979), *The Adolescent Passage.* New York: International Universities Press.

Borriello, J. (1976), Leadership in the therapist-centered group-as-a-whole psychotherapy approach. *International Journal of Group Psychotherapy, 26* 149–162.

Breen, D. (1975), *The Birth of a First Child: Towards an Understanding of Femininity.* London: Tavistock.

———. (1977), Some of the differences between group and individual therapy in connection with the therapist's pregnancy. *International Journal of Group Psychotherapy, 27,* 499–506.

Browning D. (1974), Patient's reactions to their therapist's pregnancy. *Journal of the American Academy of Child Psychiatry, 13,* 468–482.

Bychowski, G. (1956), Homosexuality and psychoses. In: *Perversions: Psychodynamics and Therapy,* ed. S. Lorand & Balint. New York: Random House.

Butts, N., & Cavenar, J. (1979), Colleagues' responses to the pregnant psychiatric resident. *American Journal of Psychiatry, 136,* 1587–1589.

Clarkson, S. (1980), Pregnancy as a transference stimulus. *British Journal of Medical Psychology, 53,* 313–317.

Cohen, M. (1966), Personal identity and sexual identity, *Psychiatry, 29,* 1–12.

Cole, D. (1980), Therapeutic issues arising from the pregnancy of the therapist. *Psychotherapy: Theory, Research, and Practice, 17,* 210–213.

Colman, A. (1969), Psychological state during first pregnancy. *American Journal of Orthopsychiatry, 39,* 788–797.

Davids, A., DeVault, S., & Talmadge, M. (1966), Psychological study of emotional factors in pregnancy. *Psychosomatic Medicine, 23,* 93–103.

Deutsch, H. (1932), Female sexuality. *International Journal of Psycho-Analysis, 14,* 34–56.

———. (1945), *The Psychology of Women, I & II.* New York: Gruen & Stratton.

Doehrman, M. (1976), Parallel processes in supervision and psychotherapy. *Bulletin of the Menninger Clinic, 40,* 9–104.

Doty, B. (1967), Relationships among attitudes in pregnancy and other maternal characteristics. *Journal of Genetic Psychology, 111,* 203–217.

Durkin, H. E. (1964), *The Group in Depth.* New York: International Universities Press.

———. (1981), The technical implications of general system theory for group psychotherapy. In: *Living Groups: Group Psychotherapy and General System Theory,* ed. J. E. Durkin, New York: Brunner/ Mazel, pp. 172–198.

Eisenbud, R.-J. (1982), Early and later determinants of lesbian choice. *Psychoanalytic Review, 69,* 85–109.

Eissler, K. (1953), The effect of the structure of the ego on psychoanalytic technique. *Journal of the American Psychoanalytic Association, 1,* 104–143.

Ekstein, R., & Wallerstein, R. (1958), *The Teaching and Learning of Psychotherapy.* New York: Basic Books.

Entwisle, D., & Doering, S. (1981), *The First Birth: A Family Turning Point.* Baltimore, MD: Johns Hopkins University Press.

Ezriel, H. (1950), A psychoanalytic approach to group treatment. *British Journal of Medical Psychology,* 23:59–74.

Fenichel, O. (1934), Further light on the preoedipal phase in girls. In: *Collected Papers,* ed. H. Fenichel & D. Rapaport. New York: Norton, 1953.

———. (1941), *Problems of Psychoanalytic Technique.* New York: Psychoanalytic Quarterly.

Fenster, S. (1982), [Interviews with twenty-two pregnant therapists]. Unpublished raw data.

———. (1983), Intrusion in the analytic space: The pregnancy of the psychoanalytic therapist. *Dissertation Abstracts International.* (University Microfilms No. 83–17, 555.)

Foulkes, S. H. (1964), *Therapeutic Group Analysis.* New York: International Universities Press.

Freud, A. (1958), Adolscence. *The Psychoanalytic Study of the Child, 13,* 255–278. New York: International Universities Press.

Freud, S. (1905), Three essays on the theory of sexuality. *Standard Edition, 7,* 135–243. London: Hogarth Press, 1953.

———. (1910), Leonardo da Vinci and a memory of his childhood. *Standard Edition, 11,* 3–137. London: Hogarth Press, 1957.

———. (1919), A child is being beaten. *Standard Edition, 17,* 179–204. London: Hogarth Press, 1955.

———. (1921), Group psychology and the analysis of the ego. *Standard Edition, 18,* 69–143. London: Hogarth Press, 1955.

———. (1933), The psychology of women: New introductory lectures on psychoanalysis, *Standard Edition*, *22*, 5–182. London: Hogarth Press, 1964.

Gediman, H., & Wolkenfeld, F. (1980), The parallel phenomenon in psychoanalysis and supervision: Its reconsideration as a triadic system. *Psychoanalytic Quarterly*, *49*, 234–255.

Gibbard, G., & Hartman, J. (1973), The significance of utopian fantasies in small groups. *International Journal of Psychotherapy*, *23*, 125–147.

Gill, M. (1984), Psychoanalysis and psychotherapy, a revision, *International Review of Psychoanalysis*, *11*, 161–179.

Gillman, R. (1980), Dreams in which the analyst appears as himself. In: *The Dream in Clinical Practice*, ed. J. M. Natterson, New York: Aronson.

Golombek, H., & Garfinkel, B., eds. (1983), *The Adolescent and Mood Disturbance*. New York: International Universities Press.

Goodwin, J. M. (1980), The patient's recognition of the therapist's pregnancy. *Psychiatric Annals*, *10*, 505–507.

Greenson, R. (1968), Dis-identifying from mother: Its special importance for the boy. *International Journal of Psycho-Analysis*, *49*, 370–374.

————. (1971), The real relationship between patient and psychoanalyst. In: *Explorations in Psychoanalysis*, ed. R. Greenson. New York: International Universities Press, 1978, pp. 425–440.

————. (1972), *The Technique and Practice of Psychoanalysis*. (Vol. 1). New York: International Universities Press.

———— & Wexler, M. (1969), The non-transference relationship in the psychoanalytic situation. *International Journal of Psycho-Analysis*, *50*, 27–39.

Grimm, E. (1961), Psychological tension in pregnancy. *Psychosomatic Medicine*, *23*, 520–527.

———— & Venet, W. (1966), The relationship of emotional adjustment and attitudes to the course and outcome of pregnancy. *Psychosomatic Medicine*, *28*, 34–49.

Gunther, M. S. (1976), The endangered self: A contribution to the understanding of narcissistic determinants of countertransference. *The Annual of Psychoanalysis*, *4*, 201–223. New York: International Universities Press.

Hannett, F. (1949), Transference reactions to an event in the life of the analyst. *Psychoanalytic Review*, *36*, 69–81.

Hooke, J., & Marks, P. (1962), MMPI characteristics of pregnancy. *Journal of Clinical Psychology*, *18*, 316–317.

Ingber, P. (1981, May), Paper presented at the American Psychiatric Association Annual Meeting.

Jacobson, E. (1961), Adolescent moods and the remodeling of psychic structures in adolescence. *The Psychoanalytic Study of the Child*, 16, 164-183. New York: International Universities Press.

Jarrahi-Zadeh, A., Kane, F., Van DeCastle, R., Lachenbruch, P., & Ewing, J. (1969), Emotional and cognitive changes in pregnancy and early puerperium. *British Journal of Psychiatry*, 115, 797-805.

Katz, J. (1978), A psychoanalyst's anonymity: Fiddler behind the couch. *Bulletin of the Menninger Clinic*, 42, 520-524.

Kernberg, O.F. (1975), *Borderline Conditions and Pathological Narcissism*. New York: Aronson.

Kissen, M. (1976), The concept of identification: an evaluation of its current status and significance for group psychotherapy. In: *From Group Dynamics to Group Psychoanalysis: Therapeutic Applications of Group Dynamic Understanding*, ed. M. Kissen. New York: Wiley.

Klein, M. (1954), *The Psychoanalysis of Children*. London: Hogarth Press.

————. (1957), *Envy and Gratitude*. London: Tavistock.

Krohn, A. (1974), Borderline empathy and differentiation of object representations: A contribution to the psychology of object relations. *International Journal of Psychiatry*, 142-165.

Lauffer, M. (1964), Ego ideal and pseudo ego ideal in adolescence. *The Psychoanalytic Study of the Child*, 19: 196–221. New York: International Universities Press.

Laufer, M. (1975), Preventive Intervention in Adolescence. *The Psychoanalytic Study of the Child*, 30, 511-528. New Haven: Yale University Press.

Langs, R. (1975), The therapeutic relationship and deviations in technique. *International Journal of Psychoanalytic Psychotherapy*, 106-141.

Lax, R. F. (1969), Some considerations about transference and countertransference manifestations evoked by the analyst's pregnancy. *International Journal of Psycho-Analysis*, 50, 363-372.

Leifer, M. (1980), *Psychological Effect of Motherhood: A Study of First Pregnancy*. New York: Praeger.

Lesser, R. (1983), Supervision: Illusions, anxieties, and questions. *Contemporary Psychoanalysis*, 19, 120-129.

Light, H., & Fenster, C. (1974), Maternal concerns during pregnancy. *American Journal of Obstetrics and Gynecology*, 118, 46-50.

Little, M. I. (1951), Countertransference and the patient's response to it. *International Journal of Psycho-Analysis*, 32, 32-40.

Lubin, B., Gardener, S., & Roth, A. (1975), Mood and somatic symptoms during pregnancy. *Psychosomatic Medicine*, 37, 136-146.

Masterson, J. (1972), *Treatment of the Borderline Adolescent.* New York: Wiley.

Murai, N., & Murai, N. (1975), A study of moods in pregnant women. *Tohoku Psychological Folia, 34,*10-16.

Nacht, S. (1958), Variations in technique. *International Journal of Psycho-Analysis, 39,* 235-237.

Nadelson, C., Notman, M., Arons, E., & Feldman, J. (1974), The pregnant therapist. *American Journal of Psychiatry, 131,* 1107-1111.

Naparstek, B. (1976), Treatment guidelines for the pregnant therapist. *Psychiatric Opinion, 13,* 20-25.

Nunberg, H. (1938), Homosexuality, magic, and aggression. *International Journal of Psycho-Analysis, 19,* 1-16.

Offerman-Zuckerberg, J. (1980), Psychological and physical warning signals regarding pregnancy: Adaptation and early psychotherapeutic intervention. *Psychological Aspects of Pregnancy, Birthing, and Bonding.* ed. B. L. Blum, New York: Human Sciences Press.

Osborne, D. (1977), Comparison of MMPI scores of pregnant women and female medical patients. *Journal of Clinical Psychology, 33,* 448-450.

Paluszny, M. & Poznanski, E. (1971), Reactions of patients during the pregnancy of the psychotherapist. *Child Psychiatry and Human Development, 4,* 266-274.

Phillips, S. (1982), *Countertransference Reactions of the Pregnant Analyst.* Paper presented at Division 39, American Psychological Association Winter Meeting, Puerto Rico.

Pines, D. (1972), Pregnancy and motherhood: Interaction between fantasy and reality. *British Journal of Medical Psychology, 45,* 333-343.

———. (1982), The relevance of early psychic development to pregnancy and abortion. *International Journal of Psycho-Analysis, 63,* 311-319.

Ponton, L. (1985, October), *Adolescent Reactions to Therapist Pregnancy.* Paper presented at American Academy of Child and Adolescent Psychiatry, San Antonio, TX.

Racker, H. (1968), *Transference and Countertransference.* New York: International Universities Press.

Raphael-Leff, J. (1980), Psychotherapy with pregnant women. *Psychological Aspects of Pregnancy, Birthing, and Bonding,* ed. B. L. Blum. New York: Human Sciences Press, pp. 174-203.

Riviere, J. (1932), Jealousy as a mechanism of defense. *International Journal of Psycho-Analysis, 13,* 414-424.

Rosenfeld, H.A., (1949), Remarks on the relation of male homosexuality to paranoia, paranoid anxiety and narcissism. *International Journal of Psycho-Analysis, 30,* 36-47.

Rossi, A. (1968), Transition to parenthood. *Journal of Marriage and the Family, 30,* 26-39.

Rubin, C. (1980), Notes from a pregnant therapist. *Social Work, 25,* 210-214.

Rycroft, C. (1968), *Imagination and Reality.* New York: International Universities Press.

Scheidlinger, S. (1974), On the concept of the "Mother Group." *International Journal of Group Psychotherapy, 24,* 417-428.

Schwartz, M. (1975), Casework implications of a worker's pregnancy. *Social Casework,* Jan., 27-34.

Schwarz, C. (1980), The pregnant psychiatrist. *Psychiatric Annals, 10,* 502-504.

Searles, H. (1955), The informational value of the supervisor's emotional experiences. *Psychiatry, 18,* 135-146.

Segal, H. (1964), *Introduction to the Work of Melanie Klein.* New York: Basic Books.

Socarides, C. W. (1978), *Homosexuality.* New York: Aronson.

Spence, D. (1973), Tracing a thought stream by computer. In: *Psychoanalysis and Contemporary Science* (Vol. 2) ed. B. Rubinstein. New York: Macmillan.

Stoller, R. (1974), Facts and fancies: an examination of Freud's concept of bisexuality. In: *Women and Analysis,* ed. J. Strouse, New York: Grossman.

Stoller, R.J. (1975), *Perversion: The Erotic Form of Hatred.* New York: Dell.

Stone, L. (1961), *The Psychoanalytic Situation.* New York: International Universities Press.

Tarnower, W. (1966), Extra-analytic contacts between the psychoanalyst and the patient. *Psychoanalytic Quarterly, 35,* 399-413.

Titus-Maxfield, M., & Maxfield, R. (1979), *Pregnancy of the Psychotherapist: Implications for Treatment.* Unpublished manuscript.

Tobin, S. (1957), Emotional depression in pregnancy. *Obstetrics and Gynecology, 10,* 677-681.

Turrini, P. (1980), Psychological crises in normal pregnancy. In: *Psychological Aspects of Pregnancy, Birthing, and Bonding* (Vol. IV), ed. B. L. Blum & P. Olsen. New York: Human Sciences Press.

Underwood, M. & Underwood, E. (1976), Clinical observations of a pregnant therapist. *Social Work, 21,* 512-517.

van Leeuwen, K. (1966), Pregnancy envy in the male. *International Journal of Psycho-Analysis, 47,* 319-324.

Weiss, S. (1975), The effects on the transference of 'special events' occurring during psychoanalysis. *International Journal of Psycho-Analysis, 56*, 69-75.

Westbrook, M. (1978), The effect of the order of a birth on a woman's experience of childbearing. *Journal of Marriage and the Family, 40*, 165-172.

Winnicott, D. W. (1956), Primary maternal preoccupation. In: *Through Pediatrics to Psycho-Analysis*, ed. D. W. Winnicott. New York: Basic Books, 1975.

————. (1963), Dependence in infant-care, in child-care, and in the psychoanalytic setting. *International Journal of Psycho-Analysis, 44*, 339-344.

Winokur, G., & Werboff, J. (1956), The relationship of conscious maternal attitudes to certain aspects of pregnancy. *Psychiatric Quarterly Supplement, 30*, 61-73.

Wolf, A. (1950), The psychoanalysis of groups. *American Journal of Psychotherapy, 4*, 16-50.

———— Schwartz, E., McCarty, G. & Goldberg, I. (1972), Psychoanalysis in groups: contrasts with other group therapies. In: *Progress in Group and Family Therapy*, eds. C. J. Sager & H. S. Kaplan. New York: Bruner/Mazel.

Wolstein, B. (1981), The psychic realism of psychoanalytic inquiry. *Contemporary Psychoanalysis, 17*, 399-412.

Author Index

Subject Index